SAUSSURE
and
Contemporary Culture

HUTCHINSON RADIUS

SAUSSURE
AND
CONTEMPORARY
CULTURE

Françoise Gadet

Translated by Gregory Elliott

HUTCHINSON RADIUS

An imprint of Century Hutchinson Ltd
62-65 Chandos Place, London WC2N 4NW

Century Hutchinson Australia (Pty) Ltd
89-91 Albion Street, Surry Hills,
New South Wales 2010, Australia

Century Hutchinson New Zealand Limited
PO Box 40-086, Glenfield, Auckland 10,
New Zealand

Century Hutchinson South Africa (Pty) Limited
PO Box 337, Bergvlei 2012, South Africa

First English edition published by Hutchinson Radius 1989
First published by
PUF 1986

British Library Cataloguing in Publication Data

Gadet, Françoise
  Saussure and contemporary culture.
  1. Linguistics. Theories of Saussure, Ferdinand de, 1857-1913
  I. Title
  410.′92′4

ISBN 0-09-182326-9

Printed and bound in Great Britain by
Anchor Press Ltd, Tiptree, Essex

Contents

Abbreviations

CGL   Ferdinand de Saussure, *Course in General Linguistics* (trans. Wade Baskin, Fontana, London 1974)

CLG   Ferdinand de Saussure, *Cours de linguistique générale* (critical edition prepared by Tullio de Mauro, Payot, Paris 1972)

EC   Rudolf Engler, *Edition critique du Cours de linguistique générale* (Otto Harrassowitz, Wiesbaden 1967–74)

SM   Robert Godel, *Les Sources manuscrites du Cours de linguistique générale* (Droz, Geneva 1957)

WUW   Jean Starobinski, *Words upon Words: The Anagrams of Ferdinand de Saussure* (Yale University Press, New Haven 1979)

IPM   Théodore Flournoy, *Des Indes à la planète Mars* (Seuil, Paris 1983)

CFS   *Cahiers Ferdinand de Saussure* (Geneva, 1941–   )

Translator's Note

As Françoise Gadet herself notes (p. 139), the fundamental Saussurian distinction betwen *langage* (the faculty of language, realized in languages), *langue* (the language system), and *parole* (individual manifestations of language, whether written or spoken), poses considerable difficulties of translation in English. In the standard 1959 translation of Saussure's *Cours de linguistique générale* by Wade Baskin, *langage* is rendered as 'speech', *langue* as 'language' and *parole* as 'speaking' – an unsatisfactory solution. The recent translation by Roy Harris (Duckworth, 1983), on the other hand, differs so radically from its predecessors on numerous points, that to have employed its controversial terminology would risk rendering Gadet's commentary incomprehensible.

I have therefore adopted the following procedure. All quotations from the *Cours* have been cited from the revised edition of the Baskin translation published by Fontana in 1974; other than restoring one or two omissions from the original French, the only systematic modification that has been made to the text is the insertion of *langue*, *parole* and *langage* in square brackets, as and when appropriate. Otherwise, for stylistic and conceptual reasons, these terms have generally been left untranslated in the remainder of the book. Whenever the word 'language' does figure, its referent (*langage* or *langue*) will be found in square brackets alongside it if there is any ambiguity.

Non-specialist readers will find Oswald Ducrot and Tzvetan Todorov's *Encyclopedic Dictionary of the Sciences of Language* (Basil Blackwell) an invaluable guide to unfamiliar linguistic terms.

I am grateful to Ann Scott for advice on particular points; to David Macey for his numerous improvements and corrections at the copy-editing stage; and especially to Sarah Baxter, who found the time to help throughout.

Gregory Elliott

1

SAUSSURE: A SCIENCE OF LANGUAGE

1

An Unusual Master

Saussure is still read today. Frequent reprints of the *Course in General Linguistics* (henceforth CGL) are sufficient testimony: 1922, 1931, 1949, 1955; a further five between 1955 and 1963 (20,000 copies); and twenty-three between 1964 and 1985 (150,000 copies). To these must be added numerous translations. All the evidence suggests that people working in and around the subject of linguistics continue to read and discuss a work that dates from 1916. Given that linguistics is a recent discipline in which models succeed one another rapidly, the CGL's survival seventy years after its first appearance is no trivial matter. So the first thing to say is that the CGL is still read.

There are pedagogical readings: the majority of linguistics teachers believe that an introduction to the subject one way or another involves reading the CGL. There are also scientific readings, for most of the major works of twentieth-century linguistics have attended to Saussure's propositions, endorsing them or suggesting modifications or rejection.[1] And then there are readings which might be called philosophical, concerned as they are with issues of language [*langue et langage*] that transcend the preoccupations of linguists.[2]

The mere name of Saussure divides linguists into supporters and opponents. For Saussure are the structuralists, adherents of a linguistic current whose analysis of *langue* as a system claims to be based upon the CGL. There are the numerous linguists who, regardless of whether they are structuralists, derive decisive ideas about the nature and functioning of

11

language [*langue*] from it. Likewise pro-Saussure are those who salute a founder, even if they at once add that he has been superseded – among them Chomsky, who, in a country where Saussure has largely been ignored, has the exceptional merit of returning to him.[3] Against Saussure are all those who believe that his concepts have had the effect of inhibiting or arresting the development of linguistics (they therewith concede his influence). Also antagonistic are those who counterpose to the Saussure of the CGL the Saussure concerned with questions of poetics.[4] These frequently violent conflicts demonstrate that the CGL remains the site of a controversy: can modern linguistics be said to have commenced with it? If so, in what sense?

The fact that Saussure's theory and method today appear to have been abandoned as such by a large number of linguists does not mean that Saussurian thought is obsolete, either in linguistics or philosophy and the human sciences. What is essential in Saussure, transcending any particular linguistic practice?

Saussure shows that man is not the master of his language. By questioning self-evident grammatical facts and their functioning for the speaking subject, he helped to wrest reflection on language from the empirically obvious. In studying *langue* as an abstract object – a system whose mechanisms are external both to the individual and physical reality – Saussurian theory contributed to the deconstruction of the free and conscious psychological subject dominant in philosophical thought and the nascent human sciences at the end of the nineteenth century. One can see why Saussure has been associated with Freud, Marx, Darwin or Copernicus.

As a result of its reflections on *langue*, Saussure's work is of the utmost interest to philosophy and the human sciences. But Saussure was above all a *linguist*: his experience and the foundations of his thought on the linguistic derive from his work on the grammar of various languages.

Anyone wishing to speak of Saussure is immediately confronted by a lacuna. Little is known of his life beyond a few dates, places and facts. He was born in Geneva in 1857 into a Protestant family of intellectuals and scientists descended from

12

eighteenth-century French immigrants. He left Switzerland to study linguistics at Leipzig in Germany, where the masters of historical linguistics taught. At this time, to be a linguist was to practise historical and comparative linguistics, which had experienced a remarkable flowering in the nineteenth century. At the end of the previous century the genetic link between Sanskrit, Greek and Latin and most of the European languages had been discovered. Research first developed on Indo-European languages, since they possessed ancient written documents. The beginning of the nineteenth century saw the establishment of the laws of phonetics with Grimm's laws (1822), which highlighted the relationship between the Germanic languages and Latin, Greek and Sanskrit. By the time Saussure appeared on the scene, the dominant linguistic school was that of the German neo-grammarians, who sought to establish the regularity of phonetic change.

In Leipzig in 1878 Saussure defended his *Mémoire sur le système primitif des voyelles dans les langues indo-européennes*, which earned him the greatest renown he was to enjoy in his own lifetime[5] – and plain incomprehension from a section of the scientific community.[6] Four years later, he defended his thesis, *De l'emploi du génitif absolu en sanscrit* – apparently a less brilliant work than the *Mémoire*.

In 1881 Saussure settled in Paris and taught at the Ecole des Hautes Etudes, first as 'senior lecturer in Gothic and Old High German' and then, from 1887 onwards, as senior lecturer in Indo-European linguistics. That he was an outstanding and scrupulous teacher is attested by several accounts, including one by Antoine Meillet, destined to become a master of French historical linguistics:

> He made us love and appreciate the science he taught; his poetic way of thinking often imparted to his account an unforgettable form full of imagery. . . He never seemed to bring a ready-made truth to his lectures; he carefully prepared everything he wanted to say, but his ideas only assumed final shape as he spoke . . . the listener would be hooked on his thought as it unfolded before him. . .
> (Quoted in CLG, p. 336)

In addition, Saussure was active in linguistic circles, and as a member of the Linguistic Society gave papers and contributed notes and reports.

In 1891 he declined a position at the Collège de France, and returned to Geneva to teach Sanskrit, Greek and Latin, Indo-European languages, modern French phonology, French versification, German literature and general linguistics.[7] He gradually retreated into silence, working intensively but publishing nothing. We know little of his last twenty-one years in Geneva. He died near the city in 1913.

We possess very few writings by Saussure. A *Recueil des publications scientifiques de F. de Saussure* appeared in 1922. His *Mémoire* and *Thèse* take up 340 of its 599 pages. The remainder consists of a series of articles, some of them very brief, on highly specialized and erudite subjects. These originally appeared in specialist reviews, with notable infrequency from 1893 onwards (Saussure published only five pieces between 1900 and 1912). Clearly, the explanation for Saussure's scientific prestige – which has earned him the title 'father' or 'founder' of modern linguistics – is not to be found here. Yet this exhausts his published writings, and alongside the 'epistolophobia' for which he reproached himself (in a letter to Meillet), one might speak of a veritable 'graphophobia' on Saussure's part.

Saussure may be universally known for his CGL, but he did not write it. He simply taught three courses in general linguistics in 1907, 1908–9 and 1910–11. After his death, two young Genevan teachers, Charles Bally and Albert Séchehaye, assumed the burden of going through such writings as he had left behind ('As soon as they had served their purpose, F. de Saussure destroyed the rough drafts of the outlines used for his lectures' – Preface to the CGL, p. xxxix), collecting the notes taken at the time by his students (there weren't many notes, as few students attended the lectures), and constructing a book out of them – the *Cours de linguistique générale*.

Later, we shall discuss some of the difficulties they encountered. Over the years, various researchers have attempted to reconstruct the editors' itinerary. In 1957 Robert Godel published *Les Sources manuscrites du Cours de linguistique générale*. Between 1967 and 1974 five instalments of Rudolf Engler's

Edition critique du Cours de linguistique générale de Ferdinand de Saussure appeared, containing the sources for each segment. And in the Italian translation of the CGL (1967) Tullio de Mauro supplied numerous notes summarizing the sources, commentaries and critiques.[8] These works compare the end-product and the materials from which it was constructed, and it is now impossible to read the CGL without taking account of them. To read the CGL is no longer a matter of just reading the CGL.

There is, however, another dimension to Ferdinand de Saussure. His intellectual interests were not confined to works for a specialist audience and three courses on general linguistics written by other hands. Although few traces of it survive, we know that for a time Saussure was seized by a passion which seems at the very antipodes of scientific reason. The dichotomy is now commonly referred to by the metaphor of day and night: the official path of the CGL and the dark side of unavowed research. Whatever its drawbacks, the metaphor facilitates examination of the relationship between the 'two Saussures'.

When Jean Starobinski published *Words upon Words* in 1971, presenting Saussure's thoughts on anagrams, some went so far as to speak of a 'second Saussurian revolution'.[9] What did it involve? Between 1906 and 1909, when the first courses in general linguistics were in gestation, Saussure thought he had discovered the traces of an esoteric poetic activity in Saturnian Latin verse which he termed anagrams. He believed that another text was inscribed in the interior of the poem (*under* the text, so to speak). The relationship between the two could be described as follows. A 'theme' of a few words, generally a proper noun, gives rise to a number of phonic fragments. The poem is composed in such a way as to comprise the maximum possible number of such fragments. For example:

Taurasia   *CI*sauna   Samn*IO*   ce*PI*t   >   SCIPIO

Saussure progressively extended his researches to Greek and Latin epic, lyric and dramatic poetry, and then to Latin prose. He discovered a 'stream' of anagrams wherever he turned. Convinced that their abundance indicated a conscious operation on the writer's part, he asked a contemporary composer of Latin poetry whether anagrams occurred in his work 'deliberately or by chance' (WUW, p. 119). When the poet did not reply, Saussure abandoned his labours, which had filled something approaching 140 notebooks, without publishing a thing.

Work on the Germanic legends of the *Niebelungen* can either be attributed to a diurnal or a nocturnal Saussure. It led to some teaching in 1904, but although he planned to write a book, nothing out of eighteen notebooks appeared in print. Saussure's research consisted in charting the various reformulations of a legend, examining the symbolic status of its constitutive elements, as new versions increased the distance from the historical event at its source.

The most striking evidence of a second Saussure lies elsewhere, in the Genevan psychiatrist Théodore Flournoy's book, *Des Indes à la planète Mars* (1900), which describes a case of glossolalia (the gift of tongues, or conversing in an invented language). Saussure is mentioned twenty-five times as a Sanskrit expert in a chapter devoted to the supposedly Hindu language of the clairvoyant, Mlle Smith. This is because a fair proportion of it is composed of extracts from Saussure's letters to Flournoy. Since Saussure himself wrote nothing on the subject these traces in someone else's work constitute our only source of information on what induced him to take an interest in spiritualist seances, to attempt to uncover the link between this putative Hindu and Sanskrit, in the years 1895–8.

What is the connection between this research and the CGL? Here the metaphor of day and night ceases to be fruitful, suggesting as it does a divided Saussure, whereas we shall seek to capture the underlying consistency of his enterprise.

So the 'Master of Geneva' did not write. If Saussure's name has come to represent something, it is because others did. Today, accordingly, it seems impossible to approach his work except as a circulation of writings – from the sources and the CGL to the commentaries by Godel, Engler and Mauro, and the responses which the CGL has not ceased to provoke.

The reading which follows aims to take this circulation of texts into account. But the CGL will remain in the forefront of our study, which will not attempt a historical restoration (rediscovery of the Master's authentic thought or explanation of his intentions). In the last analysis, whatever comments may be made about the work of its editors, the CGL as established by them is the founding document of structuralism – from its inception in linguistics to the borrowings and reconstructions it has undergone in philosophy and the human sciences. It is the CGL that has been adopted, commented upon, discussed, refuted, and frequently misunderstood – but which has influenced one thinker after another.

Sticking to the text of the CGL does not condemn us to the vulgage[10] – a term now commonly applied to the CGL and interpretations of it which ignore its confused, contradictory or problematic aspects. The extent to which this vulgate has coarsened or frozen Saussure's thought, elevated the CGL into an inviolable object, mystified the character of Saussure, and repudiated the remainder of his work, cannot be overemphasized.

Yet such readings have become rare since the research on the sources, and especially since the 1960s. Ours will be concerned with the theoretical totality, proceeding on the assumption that the whole theoretical apparatus coheres and that its concepts are inter-related. All too often introductions to Saussure expound his concepts in isolation: *langue/parole*, sign/signifier/signified, synchrony/diachrony, syntagm/paradigm, system and value, etc. etc. But how are these related? The supposition that they are is at stake in a comprehensive reading.

What follows is also informed by a 'philological' interest in the genesis of a work constructed from heteroclite sources, which only offer access to Saussure's work via a set of 'traces'. In so far as they provide insight into its genesis, following Godel and Engler we shall revert to them.

Only an internal reading will be attempted here, where the focus will be the foundation of an intellectual position in linguistics to which we wish to accord a contemporary relevance. In Part Two, we will proceed to a historical reading, examining Saussure's relationship to his contemporaries, predecessors, disciples, opponents, editors, readers and commentators.

Finally, this will be a personal reading – my reading. Whilst it seeks to avoid overly adventurous interpretations, it does not exclude my own interests. This explains certain imbalances in the exposition (more space is devoted to system and mechanism, for example, than to the sign). Hence what follows might be characterized as a *linguistic* reading (there are also semiological readings, philosophical readings, historical readings, etc.). It reveals Saussure to be more innovatory than is generally supposed.

2

How the *Course in General Linguistics* was Constructed

Letter to Meillet of 1894

But I am heartily sick of it all and of the general difficulty of writing even ten lines of common sense on linguistic matters. For a long time I have been particularly concerned with classifying linguistic facts and the viewpoints from which we treat them. And I am more and more aware both of the enormous amount of work necessary to show the linguist *what he is doing*, by reducing each operation to its appropriate category, and of the ultimate futility of what can be accomplished in linguistics.

Ultimately, the only aspect of a language that interests me is its picturesque or quasi-ethnographic side – what distinguishes it from others as the property of a particular people with certain origins. But I have lost the pleasure of unreservedly devoting myself to such study and appreciating a particular fact pertaining to a particular milieu.

The utter inadequacy of current terminology, the necessity of reforming it and, in order to do that, of demonstrating what sort of object language [*langue*] is, continually spoils my pleasure in philology, even though I have no dearer wish than not to have to concern myself with the nature of language in general.

Reluctant as I may be, this will result in a book in which I shall explain, without passion and without enthusiasm, why there is not a single term in use in contemporary linguistics which has the slightest meaning for me. Only then, I confess, shall I be able to resume my work where I left off.

(Quoted from CFS 21)

SAUSSURE AND CONTEMPORARY CULTURE

Interview with Gautier, 6 May 1911

. . . I am still very bothered about my course in general linguistics. (*I tell him that people would very much like to know something at least of his philosophy of language.*) I don't think so. It's insufficiently elaborated. (*I ask him whether this had been one of his interests prior to Wertheimer's death.*) – On the contrary, I don't think I've added anything since then. It's a subject which preoccupied me above all before 1900. This year I've spoken about a lot of questions extraneous to linguistics. I started on that this winter; but it's scarcely sufficient. I find myself in a dilemma. Either I expound the subject in all its complexity and admit my doubts – which is inappropriate for a course on a subject in which there is going to be an examination. Or I do something simplified, better suited to an audience of students who aren't linguists. But at each stage I'm inhibited by scruples. To sort it out I'd need to devote months to thinking about it.

At the moment general linguistics seems like a system of geometry, resulting in theorems requiring proof. Yet one notes that theorem 12 is the same as theorem 33 in another form.

First truth: *langue* is distinct from *parole*. This only serves to disentangle the problem from anything physiological. There then remains a purely psychological matter. Now, it seems to me that one can arrive at this first prerequisite from several opposing directions. (*Here my memory fails me.*) Next, yes, what is essential is the problem of units. *Langue* is strictly comparable to a line whose components are cut up with scissors – snip, snip, snip – and not in such a way that each has a form. What are these? Etc. etc.?

(*I asked him if he had written down his ideas on the subject.*) – Yes, I have made some notes, but they're scattered all over the place in bits and pieces; I wouldn't be able to find them. (*I had intimated that he should publish something.*) – It would be absurd to embark upon lengthy research for the sake of publication when I have so very many unpublished works over there (*he gestures*). (Quoted in SM, p. 30)

For a moment let us imagine a Saussure free of graphophobia: had he written a book elaborating his thoughts on general linguistics, it is conceivable that it would have resembled his

20

other scientific texts and not have had the impact of the CGL. Hence it is worthwhile examining the history of this text.

In the Preface Bally and Séchehaye explain their selection. First of all, they had to carry out a critical examination of the students' notes, comparing occasionally divergent versions of each of the three courses point by point. Aware of the difficulty of transcribing a spoken text, they renounced the idea of publishing everything. They likewise rejected the options of only editing one of the courses, since the syllabus was not identical from one year to the next and interesting things would have been sacrificed, or of simply publishing selections, which would have obscured any coherent development. They adopted a 'bolder' solution ('to attempt a reconstruction, a synthesis, by using the third course as a starting point and by using all other materials at our disposal' – p. xxx), while acknowledging the limitations of their enterprise.

In its final form their 317-page work comprises five parts: an Introduction (setting out the problems surrounding the object of linguistics), with an appendix on phonology; Part One, devoted to 'General Principles' (wherein the sign and synchrony are examined); Part Two on 'Synchronic Linguistics', whence derive all the ideas concerning the determination of the unit, identity, the system, value, relations and mechanism; Part Three – 'Diachronic Linguistics' – devoted to changes, analogy and folk etymology (with an appendix to Parts 2 and 3); and finally, Parts Four ('Geographical Linguistics') and Five ('Concerning Retrospective Linguistics'), about which we shall have very little to say here.

Exactly what resources were at the editors' disposal? Godel itemizes them as follows:

– Notes in Saussure's hand,[1] a high proportion of which were written around 1894 – the year in which he was preoccupied with general linguistics (cf. the letter to Meillet) and probably even sketched out a book. Likewise dating from 1894 are seventy pages of notes for a tribute to the American linguist Whitney, who died that year. Saussure was planning to take the opportunity to expound his own ideas, but in the end did not even reply to the secretary of the American association. Some of these notes have been lost or destroyed.

21

– Preparatory notes for the three courses. They are brief and few in number, corresponding only to a few lectures.

– Notes taken by the students during the three courses, whose content, plan and form were different. The editors attempted to collect all the available notebooks – a feasible undertaking, given that the audience for the third course, for example, was no more than four or five.

So much for the sources. In their respective studies Godel and Engler have presented them as follows:

– After charting Saussure's relationship to general linguistics, Robert Godel's *Les Sources manuscrites du Cours de linguistique générale* (1957) describes all the materials from which the CGL was constructed and offers an extended commentary on the principal problems of Interpretation.

– Rudolf Engler's *Édition critique* contains a text divided into six columns. In the left-hand column is the text of the CGL itself, broken up into small fragments numbered 1 to 3281. Columns B, C and D contain the sources known to the editors, supplying the identifiable source for each fragment in the student notebooks (with a system of cross-references enabling any reader who so wishes to follow the source continuously). Columns E and F contain texts unknown in 1916 and rediscovered by Godel (e.g., another student notebook and some notes).[2]

Thanks to Engler's labours, it is possible to retrace the text's history – from Saussure's oral exposition to the notes taken by his students, from the editors' reading of these notes to the composition of the CGL. It only remains to evaluate the respective influence of these successive transmissions on the end-product.[3]

The structure of the book was based upon the third course, although the same overall order was not preserved. The plan of Saussure's third course can be encapsulated as follows: from the diversity of languages to *langue*, and from *langue* to linguistics. The editors, on the other hand, decided to begin with *langue* and to postpone *languages and their diversity* to the end (Parts 3, 4 and 5).

The third course is the main source for the Introduction and the first, second and fourth parts. The first course is the source for the third part and the appendices. The second course was

22

used as a supplement, and is the source of a few chapters. As to Saussure's manuscript notes, the editors only used elements in the text, which was established independently of them.

The student notes were revised in such a way as to integrate them into the text, which for the most part is a very close paraphrase of them. Many of the alterations are minimal – terminological adjustments, for example, dictated by the fact that several terms only appear in the third course. The editors also clarified a few passages which were too obscure or allusive, added or substituted examples, and appended commentaries to some diagrams.

Only some of these modifications seriously call the editors' fidelity to the sources into question, ranging from a slight hardening of Saussure's thought to alteration of the order of exposition of concepts or reduction of the importance of a subject relative to what the sources indicate. Where they are of interpretative significance, they will be signalled. For now only one example will be given – the last clause of the CGL (and one of the most frequently cited): '*the true and unique object of linguistics is language* [langue] *studied in and for itself*' (p. 232). This was supplied by Bally and Séchehaye. Although not contrary to the spirit of the CGL, it accentuates exclusivism, and it is scarcely surprising that as a result numerous structuralist linguists have construed Saussurianism as excluding any dynamism from the system, any social conditioning or link with history.

Nevertheless, it is impossible to have anything but praise for the editors' work. They mostly set aside their own positions so as to immerse themselves in Saussure's thought. That they had no doubts as to their fidelity is evinced by the fact that they only changed a few points of detail in the second edition of 1922, at a time when controversy was raging over the basic concepts.

Bally and Séchehaye can be criticized for seeking to present an impeccable Saussure. They excluded anything which might appear confused or contradictory, and even anything suggestive of a thought in search of its identity. At their hands the anxious scientist tends to become a self-confident master. It is perfectly understandable that their main priority at this early stage should have been to produce a coherent body of thought. But their day has passed, and it is time to address Saussure's anxiety about general linguistics – something only possible thanks to their work. At the outset it was necessary to extricate Saussure's thought from the 'variations and irregularities characteristic of oral delivery' (CGL, Preface, p. xxxi). 'Today,' as Engler writes in his own Preface, 'research is concerned with the variations, with all the irregularities that inspire thought and make it fertile' (EC, p. x).

It is clear that Saussure's relationship with general linguistics was not an untroubled one; the letter to Meillet quoted above indicates his dissatisfaction with contemporary linguistics. He was astonished that no linguist had yet experienced 'even the vague desire to attain the degree of abstraction required to master both *what one is doing* and how it possesses a legitimacy and a raison d'être within the sciences as a whole' (note 10, CFS 12, p. 59).

Having analysed *langue* as a 'tightly-woven system' (interview with Riedlinger, 1909, quoted in SM, p. 29), Saussure also wished to endow theory with a close-knit form. The comparison which suggested itself to him was geometry. The parallel between linguistic theory and geometry illuminates a crucial problem – the order in which the theory of *langue* is to be presented: 'What makes the subject difficult is that it can be approached from various directions, like certain geometrical theorems: everything is the corollary of everything else in static linguistics. Whether one is talking of units, differences, oppositions, etc., it all comes down to the same thing' (interview with Riedlinger).[4]

Yet as so often, Saussure perceives the limits of his simile and, alongside theorems, suggests the example of aphorisms, defining them as follows: 'Neither axioms, nor principles, nor theses, but *delimitations, limits between which the truth is constantly encountered, wherever one starts from*' (SM, p. 51).

The perennial problem of order derives, then, from the material itself, and not from the method (or the absence of method). The CGL must be approached in the knowledge that it presents a thought still in search of its angle of attack. In modifying his framework from one year to the next, Saussure recreated the problems to which he referred in a note of 1894:

> Hence there is genuinely a necessary absence of any starting-point, and if a reader wants to follow my thought carefully from one end of this volume to the other, he will, I am sure, recognize that it was *impossible to follow a very rigorous order.*
>
> I shall take the liberty of placing the same idea before the reader as many as three or four times, because *no one point of departure is more appropriate than another as a foundation for the demonstration.* (Note 9, CFS 12)[5]

So the question of the order of presentation is coeval with Saussure's reflections. Given that it represented a problem for him and then for his editors, the reader will not be surprised to hear that it also poses a dilemma for us in this book. What order should we adopt?

The order of the CGL? We shall see the extent to which it rests upon an interpretation and even ambiguities. Since it does not correspond to the order of any of the courses, and especially not the third, there is no reason to favour it. Since it does not always spell out the theoretical links between concepts, it makes a comprehensive understanding difficult.

The order of the sources? But that would necessitate choosing between the courses and neglecting whatever is absent from the one selected.

The reconstructed order of the genesis of the concepts in Saussure's own research?[6] That would not serve for an overall understanding either.

One solution would be to attempt to unfold a logical order, taking into account the position of each concept in the general theoretical configuration. But this poses two problems. First, an interpretative problem, since the point of departure chosen is scarcely insignificant. Secondly – and even more intractably – it is not possible to unfold the CGL in linear fashion, by extracting an idea and deducing everything from it. Nor is it possible to approach any one point by a single route. A multiplicity of non-contradictory approaches contributes to the formulation of an idea engendered in several problematics at once.

Hence the solution adopted here of successive approaches which partially intersect and which cover zones of concepts, rather as though they covered a network of pathways. We will adopt both a macro and a micro approach, untroubled by possible repetition or dissipation of ideas (the synchrony/diachrony opposition, for example, is discussed in each of chapters 4, 5 and 6). Instead of establishing theses, these parallel approaches will underscore the links between the various viewpoints from which *the linguistic* is constructed.

What is Saussure's significance today? This amounts to asking what is to be expected of a linguistic theory. There are three components in any response:
– that it explain the maximum possible number of linguistic facts;
– that it account for the mechanism in the functioning of language that makes new utterances possible, in ordinary and special usages alike, in accordance with the constitutive system of each language.
– that it define the specificity of the linguist's work within the various disciplines dealing with language.

Perhaps one secret of the continuing relevance of the CGL is to be found here – in utterances that echo one another at a distance, which are not always intelligible in isolation, but which, as they intersect, suggest (rather than dictate) a conception of *langue* whose fertility readers can judge for themselves.

3

The Sign

Extract from the CGL, Part One, Chapter I

Nature of the Linguistic Sign

1. Sign, Signified, Signifier

Some people regard language [*langue*], when reduced to its elements, as a naming-process only – a list of words, each corresponding to the thing that it names. For example:

This conception is open to criticism at several points. It assumes that ready-made ideas exist before words (on this point, see below, p. 111); it does not tell us whether a name is vocal or psychological in nature (*arbor*, for instance, can be considered from either viewpoint); finally, it lets us assume that the linking of a name and a thing is a very simple operation – an assumption that is anything but true. But this rather naive approach can bring us near the truth by showing us that the linguistic unit is a double entity, one formed by the associating of two terms.

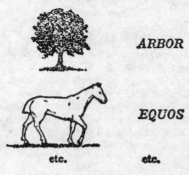

ARBOR

EQUOS

etc.   etc.

We have seen in considering the speaking-circuit (p. 11) that both terms involved in the linguistic sign are psychological and are united in the brain by an associative bond. This point must be emphasized.

The linguistic sign unites, not a thing and a name, but a concept and a sound-image.[1] The latter is not the material sound, a purely physical thing, but the psychological imprint of the sound, the impression that it makes on our senses. The sound-image is sensory, and if I happen to call it 'material,' it is only in that sense, and by way of opposing it to the other term of the association, the concept, which is generally more abstract.

The psychological character of our sound-images becomes apparent when we observe our own speech. Without moving our lips or tongue, we can talk to ourselves or recite mentally a selection of verse. Because we regard the words of our language as sound-images, we must avoid speaking of the 'phonemes' that make up the words. This term, which suggests vocal activity, is applicable to the spoken word only, to the realization of the inner image in discourse. We can avoid that misunderstanding by speaking of the *sounds* and *syllables* of a word provided we remember that the names refer to the sound-image.

The linguistic sign is then a two-sided psychological entity that can be represented by the drawing:

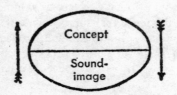

The term sound-image may seem to be too restricted inasmuch as beside the representation of the sounds of a word there is also that of its articulation, the muscular image of the phonational act. But for F. de Saussure language [*langue*] is essentially a depository, a thing received from without (see p. 13). The sound-image is par excellence the natural representation of the word as a fact of potential language [*langue*], outside any actual use of it in speaking [*parole*]. The motor side is thus implied or, in any event, occupies only a subordinate role with respect to the sound-image. [Ed.]

The two elements are intimately united, and each recalls the other. Whether we try to find the meaning of the Latin word *arbor* or the word that Latin uses to designate the concept 'tree,' it is clear that only the associations sanctioned by that language appear to us to conform to reality, and we disregard whatever others might be imagined.

Our definition of the linguistic sign poses an important question of terminology. I call the combination of a concept and a sound-image a *sign*, but in current usage the term generally designates only a sound-image, a word, for example (*arbor*, etc.). One tends to forget that *arbor* is called a sign only because it carries the concept 'tree,' with the result that the idea of the sensory part implies the idea of the whole.

Ambiguity would disappear if the three notions involved here were designated by three names, each suggesting and opposing the others. I propose to retain the word *sign* [*signe*] to designate the whole and to replace *concept* and *sound-image* respectively by *signified* [*signifié*] and *signifier* [*signifiant*]; the last two terms have the advantage of indicating the opposition that separates them from each other and from the whole of which they are parts. As regards *sign*, if I am satisfied with it, this is simply because I do not know of any word to replace it, the ordinary language suggesting no other.

The linguistic sign, as defined, has two primordial characteristics. In enunciating them I am also positing the basic principles of any study of this type.

2. Principle I: The Arbitrary Nature of the Sign

The bond between the signifier and the signified is arbitrary. Since I mean by sign the whole that results from the associating of the signifier with the signified, I can simply say: *the linguistic sign is arbitrary*.

The idea of 'sister' is not linked by any inner relationship to the succession of sounds *s-ö-r* which serves as its signifier in French; that it could be represented equally by just any other sequence is proved by differences among languages and by the very existence of different languages: the signified 'ox' has as its signifier *b-ö-f* on one side of the border and *o-k-s* (*Ochs*) on the other.

No one disputes the principle of the arbitrary nature of the sign, but it is often easier to discover a truth than to assign to it its proper place. Principle I dominates all the linguistics of language [*langue*]; its consequences are numberless. It is true that not all of them are equally obvious at first glance; only after many detours does one discover them, and with them the primordial importance of the principle.

Course in General Linguistics, Part One, Chapter I, pp. 65–8

In this chapter we shall be approaching *langue* via a question which any reflection on language or linguistic theory must address: granted, the phonic or graphic materiality of a language transmits meaning; but how is this to be explained? Answering it involves us in confronting two problems traditional in philosophy, but not considered of equal importance by linguistics:

– the relation between what is heard (sound) and what is understood (meaning). This problem is omnipresent in linguistics.

– the relation between language [*langue*] and reality – a question which linguists influenced by the Saussurian legacy bracket, since reality is excluded from their discipline.

The connection between these two issues is normally broached by means of a triangle which represents the sign as conceived in philosophy, comprising thing, word and idea. Saussure's employment of the notion of sign might suggest that he merely resumes a long tradition in the philosophy of language, dating back at least to the Stoics. However, the Saussurian sign comprises only two poles, not three: the signifier and the signified. Does this betoken the suppression of one pole, a redistribution of terms, or a transformation of the problematic itself?

1. *Langue* is not a nomenclature

In seeking to define *langue* and what constitutes it, Saussure arrives at a primarily negative conclusion: it is not to be conceived as a nomenclature. It is not defined by a bond between a thing and the term used to refer to it. Thus Saussure immediately declares against seeing *langue* as 'a list of words, each corresponding to the thing that it names' (p. 65). For this assumes the existence of a stock of things (or ideas) ready and waiting to receive their designation from a stock of labels, and that the ideas to be expressed (whether things or concepts) are already constituted prior to *langue* and conceivable without its intervention. Saussure counterposes the following description: 'Without language [*langue*], thought is a vague, uncharted nebula. There are no pre-existing ideas, and nothing is distinct before the appearance of language [*langue*]' (p. 112).

Saussure's main argument against the commonsense conception is the comparison between languages: translation does not merely involve the replacement of one term by another. Whilst the German distinguishes between *mieten* and *vermieten*, the French possesses only *louer* ('to let' and 'to rent'). The English *to know* covers both *savoir* and *connaître*. In French the distinction between *fleuve* and *rivière* is determined by whether the water flows into the sea or another river; whereas the difference between *river* and *stream* is one of size. What these examples demonstrate is that different languages do not divide up reality in the same way, that what is involved is a division [*découpage*] whose precise form is not dictated by the material substance of reality. The reality of flowing water exhibits neither *fleuve/rivière* nor *river/stream*. . .

The 'simplistic' conception of language as nomenclature helps, nevertheless, to clarify the nature of the sign. It is a two-sided entity, an association of two orders. This is the only definition of the sign in isolation offered in the CGL: 'The linguistic sign unites, not a thing and a name, but a concept and a sound-image' (p. 66). Or, in the terms adopted by Saussure from the third course onwards, the sign unites a *signifier*, 'the psychological imprint of the sound', and a *signified*, the mental representation of the meaning. 'The two elements are intimately united, and each recalls the other' (p. 66) – an indissolubility Saussure illustrates by comparing the sign to a sheet of paper with its inseparable recto and verso.

The two sides united in the sign are something pertaining to the order of the idea, the concept, the absent, on the one hand, and a material representation (phonic or graphic), on the other. There is a decisive difference between this conception and the classical representation: the exclusion of reality results in the delimitation of a domain of signs – the field of the linguistic.

Yet this exclusion does not seem to have been easy for Saussure, and because of textual contradictions it is not obvious to readers of the CGL. Thus when Saussure represents the sign by the following diagram (p. 67):

we are to understand that the top half represents the signified, the bottom half the signifier, the ellipsis delimits the sign, and the arrows indicate the indissociability of the two sides of the sign, together with the productive and receptive aspects of the speech circuit.[1] However, this representation is utterly inappropriate, for it suggests the existence, on the one hand (in the realm of the signified), of a delimited zone of reality to which the signifier *arbor* is assigned, and on the other (in that of the signifier) a signifier which is assigned to the signified   . This amounts to a return to nomenclature via a detour.

Other comments in the CGL make it clear that this is not the essence of the Saussurian conception. It is not a question of a signified and a signifier which are then united by some bond intervening subsequently. There is a bond in which both signified and signifier are created, in a sign.

The role played by the sign is now plain: it simultaneously defines an order of *langue* independent of reality and posits *langue* as the *bond* between sound and idea. This poses the question of whether the configuration of the sign is coextensive with the very idea of linguistics. This is certainly the case for Saussure. The sign is vital to the study of *langue* – which explains why he regarded linguistics as part of semiology (p. 16):

> Language [*langue*] is a system of signs that express ideas, and is therefore comparable to a system of writing, the alphabet of deaf-mutes, symbolic rites, polite fomulas, military signals, etc. But it is the most important of all these systems.
>
> *A science that studies the life of signs within society* is conceivable; it would be a part of social psychology and consequently of general psychology; I shall call it *semiology* (from the Greek *sēmeîon* 'sign'). Semiology would show what constitutes signs, what laws govern them. Since the science does not yet exist, no one can say what it would be; but it has a right to existence, a place staked out in advance. Linguistics is only a part of the general science of semiology; the laws discovered by semiology will be applicable to linguistics, and the latter will circumscribe a well-defined area within the mass of anthropological facts.

2. The arbitrariness of the sign

The primary characteristic of the sign as defined by Saussure is that it is arbitrary: 'The bond between the signifier and the signified is arbitrary' (p. 67). The definition of the arbitrariness of the sign is one of the most frequently discussed passages in the CGL, perhaps because of its proximity to an old philosophical debate. However, it should be noted that the terms of the debate are not the same. In philosophy arbitrariness characterizes the bond between a thing and its name, whereas in linguistics it is the principle according to which a signifier like [*soer*] is not bound by any 'internal' relation to the signified '*soeur*'. 'The bond uniting the signifier and the signified is radically arbitrary', we read in the *Sources*. ('Radically' is omitted from the CGL, which risks losing the sense of 'in its very roots', as well as the contrast with an unradical arbitrariness – see below on relative arbitrariness).

Saussure stresses straightaway that no-one disputes this principle. This is the more so in that many linguists interpret it as the latest instalment in the debate between naturalists and conventionalists which has marked the history of linguistics from the Greeks onwards. Naturalists hold that the origin of language is natural and that the relations between words and the things they designate are imposed by nature or by realities extraneous to humanity. Conventionalists regard language [*langue*] as a convention, a kind of implicit contract whereby such and such a meaning reverts to such and such a segment. They would regard Saussurian arbitrariness merely as a version of traditional philosophical arbitrariness, referring to the relation between words and things.

Linguists have felt able to construe Saussurian arbitrariness as a *prise de position* in this debate because of a certain confusion in the CGL. Indeed, the examples of *soeur* and of *boeuf* are introduced in an unfortunate manner ('the signified "ox" has as its signifier *b-ö-f* on one side of the border and *o-k-s* (*Ochs*) on the other', p. 68). Although unquestionably Saussure's (Course I), this formulation represents a regression towards the nomenclature criticized three pages earlier: it assumes a ready-made signified (hence one overlapping with the thing) awaiting its signifier.

If Saussure must be assigned a position in the old controversy, then he is a conventionalist; he professes total agreement with the conventionalist Whitney. Yet he is a good deal more than this, as his remark that Whitney 'did not follow through' (p. 76) the implications of the sign's arbitrariness indicates. The difference is not always explicitly stated, but is established *de facto* by Saussure's elaboration of a new theoretical system rendering its antecedent obsolete.

Saussure remains close to the philosophical debate, in so far as the arguments he uses are those of the classical dispute between naturalists and conventionalists: the viewpoint of the

omenclator, the comparison between *sign* and *symbol*, onomato-
oeias and the origins of language. Yet his position is gradually
emarcated from the classical perspective and a specifically
nguistic conception emerges:
  – The viewpoint of the nomenclator: 'We might conceive of
n act by which, at a given moment, names were assigned to
nings and a contract was formed between concepts and sound-
mages; but such an act has never been recorded. The notion
nat things might have happened like that was prompted by our
cute awareness of the arbitrary nature of the sign' (p. 71).
aussure shows that the contract cannot be historically located,
nd yet accepts the assumption. Here he is a strict convention-
list, and retreats from positions implying the assertion of
adical arbitrariness.
  – Signs are distinct from symbols, for the latter are never
uly arbitrary. In the symbol, 'there is the rudiment of a natural
ond between the signifier and the signified' (p. 68); for
xample, the symbol of justice – a pair of scales – is linked to
hat it represents. Here linguistics and philosophy coincide.
  – Onomatopoeias, interjections, and imitative harmonies are
ffered as evidence against arbitrariness by naturalists. Saussure
ejects them, since like all signs they are subject to the laws of
nguistic change. Moreover, there are onomatopoeias in Latin
hich are not such in French (*pipio* yields *pigeon*), as well as
rench onomatopoeias that do not exist in Latin (*fouet*, from
ugus, 'beech-tree'). Philosophy and linguistics once again
oncur in a conventionalist conclusion.
  – On the origin of language Saussure has no difficulty
howing that the conventionalist position involves a surreptitious
eturn to nomenclature; it assumes two previously constituted
rders upon which a convention subsequently operates in order
o effect their association. Here Saussure quits the terms of the
lassical debate, abandoning the problematic of the origin of
anguage. Language [*langue*] is not a contract pure and simple;
s far as speakers are concerned, it is 'a thing that is tolerated
nd not a rule to which all freely consent' (p. 71). 'The question
f the origin of language does not even exist. The so-called
rimitive contract merges with what happens every day. There
s no moment at which genesis differs characteristically from

the life of language, and the essential thing is to have understood the latter' (n. 12). Restoring the principle of language [*langue*] to this life, Saussure establishes it as a system of signs whose equilibrium is permanently assured by social functioning: 'the only real object of linguistics is the normal, regular life of an existing idiom' (p. 72).

The relationship between the plane of language [*langue*] and the plane of reality is another important argument in the debate over the sign and its arbitrariness. We have seen that Saussure's definition of the sign excluded reality from linguistic discussion. Hence the arbitrariness of the sign does not concern the bond between thing and name – recognized as arbitrary by any conventionalist – but the bond between signified and signifier. This presents a problem. The bond is arbitrary from the standpoint of language [*langue*] (and the linguist who describes it) but not for the speaking subject, upon whom it is imposed ('the community . . . is bound to the existing language', p. 71). It is independent of the will of speakers, for whom it is *necessary*. Accordingly, Saussure, aware of the ambiguity of the word 'arbitrary' in this respect, modifies his definition of the sign as follows: 'I mean that it is unmotivated, i.e. arbitrary in that it actually has no natural connection with the signified' (p. 69). With these three characteristics – arbitrary, necessary, unmotivated – a delimited linguistic field begins to take shape.

But the new formulation of 'arbitrary' as 'unmotivated' contains a further difficulty. For it might again suggest the existence of a signified anterior to the sign. The recurrence of the problem indicates the extent of the difficulty. So it must be reiterated that it is the arbitrary bond which, by giving birth to the sign, creates the signified as well as the signifier. To return to the simplified example of *fleuve/rivière*, we have seen that the semantic distinction between the two is not required by anything in extra-linguistic reality: they were created by a linguistic division. Hence signifieds and signifiers are simultaneously instituted by the sign. Neither plane pre-exists the sign.

Ultimately, the retroactive effect of the second part of the CGL on the definition of the sign and its arbitrariness obliges us to choose between the partially contradictory claims governing the emergence of the new terrain of linguistics along

ide the philosophical terrain which gives rise to the reflections
on the origin of language and the relation between language
[langue] and reality.

Our reading will be guided by the hypothesis that the
Saussurian model is coherent: arbitrariness in the trivial sense
does not accord with the definition of the sign as the bond of
a signifier and a signified – a definition which contains in
embryo the idea of the system, presenting signs relative to one
another (see Chapter 4).

3. From the unmotivated sign to relative arbitrariness

The interpretative problems surrounding 'unmotivated', as
opposed to 'arbitrary', indicate that we are actually dealing
with two different senses of *arbitrary*. In the first, the sense of
conventional (as opposed to natural) is determined by reference
to extra-linguistic reality. In the second, it can be paraphrased
by 'unmotivated' (as opposed to motivated) and is established
by reference to other signs.

The difference between the two is clear. The first is a philosophical problem; believing it to have been dealt with by conven-
tionalism, Saussure does not linger over it. The second suggests
the preconditions for the establishment of a specifically
linguistic terrain; the whole Saussurian enterprise is geared to
constructing this terrain through the definition of the relations
between signs. Henceforth it is understood that the linguistic
terrain is that of the second definition of arbitrary, and that the
first has been vacated.

Linguistic arbitrariness is marked by the intervention of the
second characteristic of the sign, which only applies to the
signifier: *the linearity of the signifier*. The CGL has little to say
about this, even though it is of decisive importance in the
inception of linguistics: 'While [this] principle is obvious, apparently linguists have always neglected to state it, doubtless
because they found it too simple ... the whole mechanism of
language depends upon it' (p. 70). The phonic signifier is linear
in so far as it unfolds in time, the graphic signifier in so far as
it unfolds in space – contrary, for example, to a road-sign in

37

the highway code, which superimposes pieces of information. Within the semiological domain this principle is specific to the linguistic. As a sign system, language [*langue*] is related to semiology; but it is not a sign system like the others. For Saussure it is distinguished from other systems by the linearity of the signifier, and any account of it must bear this in mind.

The fact that the signifier is necessarily linear is a precondition for analysis of the spoken chain, and of syntax (study of combinations in and beyond the word – see Chapter 5) in particular. The functioning of arbitrariness in the linear framework is expounded in the chapters of the CGL devoted to the language mechanism. A sign is *motivated* or *unmotivated* relative to other signs, as is clear from the presence of a third term which would be incongruous if arbitrary were being defined as conventional: the *relatively motivated*. 'The fundamental principle of the arbitrariness of the sign does not prevent our singling out in each language what is radically arbitrary, i.e. unmotivated, and what is only relatively arbitrary' (p. 131).

The CGL only offers a brief exposition of the relatively motivated. But the examples given are unequivocal:

For instance, both *vingt* 'twenty' and *dix-neuf* 'nineteen' are unmotivated in French, but not in the same degree, for *dix-neuf* suggests its own terms and other terms associated with it (e.g. *dix* 'ten', *neuf* 'nine', *vingt-neuf* 'twenty-nine', *dix-huit* 'eighteen', *soixante-dix* 'seventy', etc.). Taken separately, *dix* and *neuf* are in the same class as *vingt*, but *dix-neuf* is an example of relative motivation. The same is true of *poirier* 'pear-tree', which recalls the simple word *poire* 'pear' and, through its suffix, *cerisier*, 'cherry-tree', *pommier* 'apple-tree', etc. For *frêne* 'ash', *chêne* 'oak', etc. there is nothing comparable. Again, compare *berger* 'shepherd', which is completely unmotivated, and *vacher* 'cowherd', which is relatively motivated. In the same way, the pairs *geôle* 'jail' and *cachot* 'dungeon', *hache* 'ax' and *couperet* 'chopper', *concierge* 'porter' and *portier* 'doorman', *jadis* 'of old' and *autrefois* 'formerly', *souvent* 'often' and *fréquemment* 'frequently', *aveugle* 'blind' and *boiteux* 'limping', *sourd* 'deaf' and *bossu* 'hunch-backed', *second* 'second' and *deuxième* 'second (of a series)', German *Laub* and French *feuillage* 'foliage' and French *métier* 'handicraft' and German *Handwerk*. The English plural *ships* suggests through its formation the whole series *flags, birds, books,* etc., while *men* and *sheep* suggest nothing.' (pp. 131–32)

The fact that arbitrariness is relative does not put the existence of radical arbitrariness in doubt; it merely means that arbitrariness is a matter of degree. The combination *dix-sept* ('seventeen') is 'relatively motivated', but *dix* ('ten') and *sept* ('seven') remain radically arbitrary and unmotivated because they cannot be further analysed.

The definition of the sign and the assertion of its arbitrary nature enable us to enter the domain of signs (as opposed to that of things, which falls outside the scope of linguistics). The unmotivated and the relatively motivated further provide access to the domain of the relations between these signs, thanks to which language [*langue*] may be described as a system and a mechanism – restrictions upon arbitrariness (the system is the 'one respect [in which] language [*langue*] is not completely arbitrary but is ruled to some extent by logic' – p. 73).

4. Languages do and don't change

Saussure claims that the arbitrariness of the sign has numerous consequences. He refers to them whenever a notion fundamental to the functioning of *langue* is introduced, as can be seen from the following list.

List of passages in the CGL referring to the arbitrary nature of the sign:
– Before the principle is stated, when *langue* is defined ('language [*langue*] is a convention, and the nature of the sign that is agreed upon does not matter' – p. 10). (See Chapter 5.)
– When languages are characterized in relation to the time factor. They have the dual property of changing and not changing – a thesis contained in the indivisible principle of mutability/immutability (p. 71). (See below.)
– When 'value' is first broached as intrinsic to the object of

certain sciences ('science[s] concerned with values' – p. 80). (See Chapter 4.)

– In the definition of value as a relation established by *langue* between two quantities, thought and sound, which are merely shapeless and indistinct outside this linguistic relation (pp. 111–12). Arbitrariness is thus bound up with difference, for the exclusion of reality means that the sign functions in relation to other signs ('*Arbitrary and differential* are two correlative qualities' – p. 118). (See Chapter 4.)

– In the description of the role of the relatively motivated in the operation of the language mechanism (p. 131). (See Chapter 6.)

– In the characterization of phonetic change as unlimited and blind (p. 151). (See Chapters 4 and 6.)

– Finally, in the relation between analogy and relative arbitrariness (p. 161). (See Chapter 6.)

The essence of the arbitrariness of the sign consists in the assertion that nothing pertaining to the non-linguistic determines what happens in *langue*. Moreover, something peculiar to *langue* in its behaviour vis-à-vis time derives from the principle: *langue* both changes (mutability) and does not change (immutability). Indeed, the sign has no more rationale for being what it is – hence for persisting – than for being something else – hence altering.

Immutability: invariably appearing as the legacy of the previous epoch, the sign is resistant to deliberate modification. This is so for several reasons: (1) because there is no rationale for signs being what they are (a set of speakers – the linguistic community – has no cause to prefer any others); (2) because of the large number of signs making up a language; (3) because these signs constitute a system whose intrication entails that alteration of any component will affect the whole; (4) because the fact that *langue* is everyone's concern is a conserving factor.

But at the same time, mutability: there is no example of a language not altering, and 'the stream of language flows without interruption; whether its course is calm or torrential is of secondary importance' (p. 140). Whether affecting the signifier, the signified, or both, and regardless of their character, transformative factors always lead to a modification of the relation between signifier and signified. To think that the signifier alone is affected and that the signified remains stable [e.g., from the Latin *calidum* to the French *chaud* ('hot')] is, Saussure shows, to persist in a nomenclative conception of *langue*. It once again supposes a signified fixed at the outset and immune to change. The example of the Latin *necare* ('to kill'), which has yielded the French *noyer* ('to drown'), demonstates that this is not the case: the signifier, the signified, and hence the relation between the two sides of the sign and its position in the system, all undergo modification.

The characteristic mutability/immutability of *langue* derives from the arbitrariness of the sign, for *langue* – a social institution among others – is not a social institution like the others. Unlike the rest, whose elements are, to varying degrees, founded upon some natural relation or other, 'language [*langue*] is limited by nothing in the choice of means' (p. 76). There is nothing to prevent any series of sounds from being associated with any idea; any phonic element may correspond to any semantic element.

5. Is linguistics wedded to the sign?

The frequency with which the CGL refers to the arbitrary nature of the sign has led some readers to identify it as the book's cardinal principle – the key to the whole theoretical edifice and its interpretation. In the chapters that follow, we shall consider its links with the rest of Saussurian linguistics.

In order to determine its significance, we must first of all return to the role of the sign itself. This chapter began with the apparent indispensability of the sign to the study of *langue*. We must now examine whether there is an inevitable link between linguistic theory and the sign, whether the former can exist without the latter.

What role does the sign play? In Saussure, qua bond between signifier and signified, the sign represents the two poles – sound and idea – without which there would be no *langue*. And this duality of *langue* as a phonetic-semantic combination (sound/

meaning) is indeed indispensable to the definition of any language. But is it solely and necessarily representable via the sign? In dispensing with the sign, a later model – Chomsky's generative grammar – demonstrates that this is not the case. In generative grammar the planes of sound and meaning are connected by the organization of grammar into levels. A grammar is conceived as providing an interface between the plane of sound (studied by phonology) and the level of meaning (studied by semantics) through the study of the sequences constituted by syntax. Albeit in different forms, the essence of what constitutes *langue* – the relation between sound and meaning – can be found in both theories: an immediate relation in the sign for Saussure, it is mediated by syntax for Chomsky, but still a relation between the two orders. So the basic concept required for a linguistic theory is not the sign, but the association between two orders. In Saussure this function is assumed by the sign, which is merely a particular instance of a more general principle.

The sign and its main property, arbitrariness, are the vehicle for a viewpoint whose ultimate goal is quite different: 'If we are to discover the true nature of language [*langue*], we must [*first of all*] learn what it has in common with all other semiological systems' (p. 17; my emphasis). As we shall see in Chapter 5, this goal is the *definition of the linguistic*, the description of 'the especially complex nature of the particular semiology called language' (EC, 1485F). The principle of the arbitrary nature of the sign is valuable for the linguistic use Saussure extracts from it, thanks to the second characteristic of the sign – the linearity of its signifier. Hence one can conclude that the sign and its properties constitute a backdrop – a precondition of linguistic reasoning.

In the appendices to Parts Two and Three, Saussure refers one last time to the principle of the arbitrariness of the sign to propose a definition of 'explanation' in linguistics. Admittedly, the passage concerns etymology; but it is applicable to linguistics in general: 'To explain means to relate to known terms, and in linguistics, *to explain a word is to relate it to other words*, for there are no necessary relations between sound and meaning' (p. 189). In total accord with the contribution made by the definition of

42

the sign to the elucidation of *langue*, this is a veritable definition of linguistics as practised since Saussure. Disencumbered of its adhesion to reality, it is the elaboration of the linguistic, the study of the internal organization of the order of signs, the explanation of the sign by means of signs. This is the construction we shall be studying in the chapters that follow.

Further Reading

CGL:
Part One, chapters I and II
Part Two, chapter VI (3)
Appendices to Parts Two and Three

Emile Benveniste, 'Nature du signe linguistique' (1939), *Problèmes de linguistique générale*, Gallimard, Paris 1966.
Rudolf Engler, 'Théorie et critique d'un principe saussurien: l'arbitraire du signe', *Cahiers Ferdinand de Saussure* 19, 1962.
Jean-Claude Milner, 'Réflexions sur l'arbitraire du signe', *Ornicar?* 5, 1975.
—, *L'Amour de la langue*, Seuil, Paris 1978.
Claudine Normand, 'L'Arbitraire du signe comme phénomène de déplacement', *Dialectiques* 1, 1973.

4

The System

Extract from the CGL, Part Two, Chapter IV

2. Linguistic Value from a Conceptual Viewpoint

When we speak of the value of a word, we generally think first of its property of standing for an idea, and this is in fact one side of linguistic value. But if this is true, how does *value* differ from *signification?* Might the two words be synonyms? I think not, although it is easy to confuse them, since the confusion results not so much from their similarity as from the subtlety of the distinction that they mark.

From a conceptual viewpoint, value is doubtless one element in signification, and it is difficult to see how signification can be dependent upon value and still be distinct from it. But we must clear up the issue or risk reducing language to a simple naming-process (see p. 65).

Let us first take signification as it is generally understood and as it was pictured on page 67. As the arrows in the drawing show, it is only the counterpart of the sound-image. Everything that occurs concerns only the sound-image and the concept when we look upon the word as independent and self-contained.

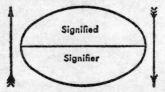

But here is the paradox: on the one hand the concept seems

44

to be the counterpart of the sound-image, and on the other hand the sign itself is in turn the counterpart of the other signs of language [*langue*].

Language [*langue*] is a system of interdependent terms in which the value of each term results solely from the simultaneous presence of the others, as in the diagram:

How, then, can value be confused with signification, i.e. the counterpart of the sound-image? It seems impossible to liken the relations represented here by horizontal arrows to those represented above (p. 114) by vertical arrows. Putting it another way – and again taking up the example of the sheet of paper that is cut in two (see p. 113) – it is clear that the observable relation between the different pieces A, B, C, D, etc. is distinct from the relation between the front and back of the same piece as in A/ A', B/B', etc.

To resolve the issue, let us observe from the outset that even outside language [*langue*] all values are apparently governed by the same paradoxical principle. They are always composed:

(1) of a *dissimilar* thing that can be *exchanged* for the thing of which the value is to be determined; and

(2) of *similar* things that can be *compared* with the thing of which the value is to be determined.

Both factors are necessary for the existence of a value. To determine what a five-franc piece is worth one must therefore know: (1) that it can be exchanged for a fixed quantity of a different thing, e.g. bread; and (2) that it can be compared with a similar value of the same system, e.g. a one-franc piece, or with coins of another system (a dollar, etc.). In the same way a word can be exchanged for something dissimilar, an idea; besides, it can be compared with something of the same nature, another word. Its value is therefore not fixed so long as one simply states that it can be 'exchanged' for a given concept, i.e. that it has this or that signification: one must also compare it with similar values, with other words that stand in opposition to it. Its content is really fixed only by the concurrence of everything that exists outside it. Being part of a system, it is endowed not only with a signification but also and especially with a value, and this is something quite different.

A few examples will show clearly that this is true. Modern French *mouton* can have the same signification as English *sheep* but not the same value, and this for several reasons, particularly because in speaking of a piece of meat ready to be served on the table, English uses *mutton* and not *sheep*. The difference in value between *sheep* and *mouton* is due to the fact that *sheep* has beside it a second term while the French word does not.

Within the same language, all words used to express related ideas limit each other reciprocally; synonyms like French *redouter* 'dread,' *craindre* 'fear,' and *avoir peur* 'be afraid' have value only through their opposition: if *redouter* did not exist, all its content would go to its competitors. Conversely, some words are enriched through contact with others: e.g. the new element introduced in *décrépit* (un vieillard *décrépit*, see p. 83) results from the coexistence of *décrépi* (un mur *décrépi*). The value of just any term is accordingly determined by its environment; it is impossible to fix even the value of the word signifying 'sun' without first considering its surroundings: in some languages it is not possible to say 'sit in the *sun*.'

Everything said about words applies to any term of language [*langue*], e.g. to grammatical entities. The value of a French plural does not coincide with that of a Sanskrit plural even though their signification is usually identical; Sanskrit has three numbers instead of two (*my eyes, my ears, my arms, my legs*, etc. are dual); it would be wrong to attribute the same value to the plural in Sanskrit and in French; its value clearly depends on what is outside and around it.

If words stood for pre-existing concepts, they would all have exact equivalents in meaning from one language to the next; but this is not true. French uses *louer* (*une maison*) 'let (a house)' indifferently to mean both 'pay for' and 'receive payment for,' whereas German uses two words, *mieten* and *vermieten*; there is obviously no exact correspondence of values. The German verbs *schätzen* and *urteilen* share a number of significations [with the French words *estimer* and *juger*], but that correspondence does not hold at several points.

46

Inflection offers some particularly striking examples. Distinctions of time, which are so familiar to us, are unknown in certain languages. Hebrew does not recognize even the fundamental distinctions between the past, present, and future. Proto-Germanic has no special form for the future; to say that the future is expressed by the present is wrong, for the value of the present is not the same in Germanic as in languages that have a future along with the present. The Slavic languages regularly single out two aspects of the verb: the perfective represents action as a point, complete in its totality; the imperfective represents it as taking place, and on the line of time. The categories are difficult for a Frenchman to understand, for they are unknown in French; if they were predetermined, this would not be true. Instead of pre-existing ideas then, we find in all the foregoing examples *values* emanating from the system. When they are said to correspond to concepts, it is understood that the concepts are purely differential and defined not by their positive content but negatively by their relations with the other terms of the system. Their most precise characteristic is in being what the others are not.

Now the real interpretation of the diagram of the signal becomes apparent. Thus

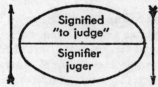

means that in French the concept 'to judge' is linked to the sound-image *juger*; in short, it symbolizes signification. But it is quite clear that initially the concept is nothing, that is only a value determined by its relations with other similar values, and that without them the signification would not exist. If I state simply that a word signifies something when I have in mind the associating of a sound-image with a concept, I am making a statement that may suggest what actually happens, but by no means am I expressing the linguistic fact in its essence and fullness.

Course in General Linguistics, Part Two, Chapter IV, pp. 114–17

The system, or mode of organization of the elements of a language at any given moment, is a fundamental notion of the CGL, and it is destined to play a crucial role in structuralism, where it goes by the name of 'structure'. It had already figured in Saussure's first work, his *Mémoire* of 1878, where, on the point of examining the *a* in Indo-European, he writes: 'The other vowels will only be considered as and when phenomena relative to the *a* arise. But if at the end of this our picture of Indo-European vocalism has been modified little by little, and if we see that it centres entirely around the *a*, adopting a new bearing on it, then clearly the whole system of vowels will in fact have come into our field of vision. . .' (p. 3). The essentials of the notion of system are already in place.

In the CGL Saussure writes: 'Language [*langue*] is a system that has its own arrangement' (p. 22). A corollary of the definition of the sign as excluding reality and as arbitrary, the idea of system permits an internal study of *langue*, involving no extraneous explanatory principles.

1. Language-state, synchrony and system

A system is an equilibrium at a given moment in the evolution of a language, a 'language-state' [*état de langue*] containing everything a speaker has at his or her disposal for speaking. Given that languages invariably evolve, time – a transformative factor – obliges linguistics to face 'two completely divergent paths' (p. 79). A distinction must be made between the axis of simultaneities (i.e., coexisting terms), termed *synchrony*, and the axis of successions, termed *diachrony*. The irreducibility of these two orders can be illustrated by the French term *pas*. The negative participle (*ne . . . pas* 'not') and the noun (*un pas* 'step') are linked diachronically (they have a common origin), but no longer synchronically (in usage).

However, synchrony is not to be taken as a mere equivalent of 'language-state' – an empirical reality which admits of discussion (does it refer to a punctual moment or a period? And if the latter, of what duration? Since *langue* is always in the process of changing, synchronic states cannot be observed:

'There are only language-states permanently in transition from the state of the day before to that of tomorrow' – SM, p. 39). Synchrony is to be understood as a concept which makes the theoretical definition of an abstract system possible (see Chapter 5).

The disjunction between state and evolution is illustrated by the metaphor of chess: 'The respective value of the pieces depends on their position on the chessboard' (p. 88) – a happy comparison in various ways. Just as a move only displaces one piece at a time, so change bears upon isolated elements. Yet this single move has the effect of altering the state of the game, and a change in one part of the system affects the whole. The diachronic fact intervenes blindly, and the subsequent synchronic consequences (modification of the system) are independent of it. Hence only the states matter, and it is not necessary to know their origin. Thus the German plural *Gäste* ('guests') once had the form *gasti*. Today all we require to grasp that *Gäste* is a plural is the couple *Gast/Gäste*. Knowing that *Gäste* has replaced *gasti* is of no advantage in using the language – any more than following the whole game provides extra information for the move underway. All the requisite information is available – on the chessboard or in the system operated by the speaker.

The comparison is flawed in one respect. The chess player moves the pieces deliberately, whereas *langue* never involves premeditation: no-one performs the role of the player.

The theoretical status of synchrony and diachrony is asymmetrical. Synchrony is preeminent, because only synchronic facts are accessible to the speaker's awareness. The essential characteristic of a synchronic fact is its capacity for creating signification. In linguistics only states have the 'power to signify: without that, *langue* would cease to be whatever it is' (SM, p. 48). To say that a particular opposition (e.g., singular/plural) is significant and available for French speakers is the same as saying that it is part of the system of French, and hence of French grammar. Therewith synchronic, systematic, significant and grammatical are rendered equivalent. The implications are three-fold:

– Speakers possess a knowledge which they employ when

they speak and which the linguist can use to establish the units of a language: 'Anything that is of even the slightest significance seems like a concrete element to them [speakers] and they never fail to single it out in discourse' (p. 106). Based on this knowledge, linguists can elaborate an analytical method still programmatic in Saussure, but which all subsequent twentieth-century linguistics has sought to develop: reliance on the 'intuition of the speaking subject'.

– Synchronic and diachronic facts are of a fundamentally different nature. In order to possess significance, a synchronic fact must connect two terms of the system ('Not *Gäste* alone but the opposition *Gast:Gäste* expresses the plural' – p. 85). By contrast, the diachronic fact affects only a single term, and the advent of a new term supposes the disappearance of the old (from *gast/gasti* to *Gast/Gäste*, a new singular/plural opposition replaces the old one).

– Synchronic work operates inside a single language – the only place where significations are constituted. Diachrony can either work on a single language or on a comparison between several.

Saussure thus dramatically inverts the relative interest in language-state and change displayed by the linguistics of his time. The comparatists were primarily interested in change. For the neogrammarians in particular, linguistics was a historical discipline, whose sole task was to study the tranformations of *langue*. Saussure does not neglect these; he is not deaf to historical linguistics, with which he was well-acquainted, which he himself practised, and which accounted for the bulk of his published work. But diachrony is allotted a secondary place in his general linguistics; evolution is the transition from one synchrony to another through the action of speaking subjects (*langue* changes via *parole* – see Chapter 5). Among diachronic facts, Saussure distinguishes between phonetic changes and analogical changes. Since the former (e.g., the transition from *calidum* to *chaud* 'hot') are never significant, they are not examined in the study of the system that is *langue*. Things are different when it comes to analogical changes (e.g., the transition from *ils preuvent* to *ils prouvent* on the model of *nous prouvons* 'prove'), as we shall see in Chapter 6.

Just as a function in a language-state does not involve any extra-linguistic volition, so for Saussure a change never supervenes for functional reasons. Saussure's conception of change is profoundly anti-teleological: 'Chance is responsible for what will become significant' (SM, p. 185). Or as Saussure writes in the CGL: 'In a fortuitous state . . . speakers took advantage of an existing difference and made it signal the distinction' (p. 85).

2. From elements to system, or from system to elements

The concept of synchrony makes it possible to define the linguist's sphere of operations: the functioning of a synchronic system.

The notion of system is ubiquitous in the CGL, at work even before it has been fully expounded. It is introduced via the comparison already cited: 'just as the game of chess is entirely in the combination of the different chesspieces, language [langue] is characterized as a system based entirely on the opposition of its concrete units' (p. 107).

The originality of the Saussurian conception of the system is evident from the steps leading up to it in linguistic thought:

1) Language [langue] possesses an organization. This is a precondition for the constitution of grammar, and has been a commonplace since Antiquity.

2) This organization assumes a particular 'form' in each language and is autonomous, based upon nothing extraneous to it. This principle underlies eighteenth- and nineteenth-century linguistics (it can be found, if not very explicitly, in Humboldt); Saussure merely adopts and systematizes it.

3) The organization takes the form of a system, a network which constitutes a form starting from phonic and semantic materials, and which possesses greater reality than the elements directly accessible in sensory experience. This is the genuinely Saussurian moment.

Contrary to comparative grammar, which takes the idea of element for granted, linguistic elements are not immediate data for Saussure: 'we must first be convinced that the concrete entities of language [langue] are not directly accessible' (p. 110).

51

Discovery of the elements and study of their functioning in the system amount to the same thing, since in order to establish them their inter-relations must be uncovered. Thus in French isolation of the *-ai-* of the imperfect (*il chant-ai-t* 'was singing') is only possible by establishing within the tense system that it is distinct from the present (*il chante*), the future (*il chante-r-a*), and the conditional (*il chante-r-ai-t*). In Saussure the system is not the sum of pre-existing elements, but the work of the relations that constitute the elements ('it is from the interdependent whole that one must start', p. 113).

Experience indicates that when we hear a foreign language spoken, it is impossible to isolate the least element in what appears a continuous chain. Saussure's starting-point is the observation that both the phonic material and the signification constitute a 'shapeless mass', within which each language makes divisions. The spoken chain appears as an unbroken thread whose units, at both the phonic and semantic levels, can only be recognized by those who know the language (and by the linguist who seeks to attain the same status). So it would seem that it is not the *substance* (phonic and/or semantic) which accounts for the language, but the *form* which the latter imposes on the substance. Examination of the substance alone would not tell us that *chanterait* must be segmented into *chante-r-ai-t* where each of the four elements has a certain meaning corresponding to a certain form. 'Language is a system whose parts can and must all be considered in their synchronic solidarity' (p. 87).

A question suggests itself: since substance cannot be relied upon, what criteria can be used to establish whether two units are identical? That the *-ai-* of *chantait* and the *-ai-* of *mangeai* ('was eating') are the same unit? Given the system, it is not enough to respond that the same signifying sequence is associated with the same signification.

In fact, to establish that two elements are identical is to show that they occupy one and the same place in the system, that they have the same value.

3. Identity, difference and value

The sources reveal that the idea of value was introduced by
Saussure at a relatively late stage, but that he became more and
more interested in it. It is not introduced as a deductive result,
but as a fundamental principle whose importance is reasserted
throughout the CGL. Saussure approaches it from several
different angles, one of which supplies a response to the question of identity.[1]

In order to define the nature of the identity of two linguistic
elements, Saussure distinguishes between two types of identity
– the material and the relational. Relational identity is that of
'two "8:25 p.m. Geneva-to-Paris" trains'. A day later, nothing
in these trains is materially identical (neither the coaches, nor
the staff, nor the passengers. . .). Yet it is the *same train*. Why?
Because its position in the system is identical relative to other
positions: this is not the Paris-Geneva train, nor the 10:15 a.m.,
nor the local Geneva-Dijon train. In contrast, material identity
is, for example, a suit which I have had stolen and subsequently
come across in a secondhand clothes shop: materially, it is
exactly the same suit. Linguistic identity is not of this nature.
On the one hand, two elements can be materially identical
without occupying the same position in the system (an oral
example is *dent* 'tooth' and *dans* 'in', both of which are
pronounced [dã]; a written example would be the verb *couvent*
'smoulder' etc. and the noun *couvent* 'convent' etc.). On the
other hand, a single term stemming from an identical relation
in the system can be represented by materially different
segments (*dans* is pronounced [dã] before a consonant and, by
elision, [dãz] before a vowel). Linguistic identity is not material,
but relational.

Let us take the various realizations of a word – *messieurs*
('gentlemen'), for example – which can vary quite considerably
from one use to another and in different situations. Whilst they
remain instances of the same word, this is not because of a
material similarity in substance, but in so far as they cannot be
reduced to another word. Thus on the phonic level, *messieurs*
is to be differentiated from *monsieur, essieu* ('axle'), *messieds*, etc.;
its pronunciation can vary within the limits established by the

existence of the other terms. The semantic level is likewise constituted by means of limits: the meaning of *messieurs* is not the same as that of *mesdames* ('ladies') or *seigneurs* ('lords'). Saussure's comment on values applies equally to linguistic elements: 'Their most precise characteristic is in being what the others are not' (p. 117). The whole system of a language is organized into *identities* and *differences*.

Unit *a* assumes its value not by virtue of its substance, but in so far as it is *not-b* or *not-c*. This is a consequence of radical arbitrariness: since the system only operates in relation to itself, 'in language there are only differences' (p. 120). But Saussure immediately adds that 'there are only differences *without positive terms*', meaning that difference has nothing primordial about it. Every term is a complex site of differences. In the German plural, for example, both *Nacht* ('night') and *Nächte* ('nights') derive their value from difference.

The subject of value is approached more clearly by way of a further comparison with chess. 'By its material make-up' (in its substance), a pawn or piece represents nothing for the player: 'it becomes a real, concrete element only when endowed with value and wedded to it'. Hence value is a relation which cannot be deciphered in the immediate evidence. One element is identical to another, whatever the realizations, 'provided the same value is attributed to it' (p. 110).

On this occasion, however, the analogy is less successful, for linguistic value is undoubtedly a particularly complex phenomenon, to which the chess simile does less than justice. In chess the number of squares is finite, unlike the potential uses of a language. Moreover, infringement of the rules is impossible (it results in the player's disqualification), whereas when people fail to respect one linguistic rule, they are in fact obeying another (e.g., when a child creates *viendre* from *viendrai* 'I shall come' on the model of *éteindre/éteindrai* 'to put out'/'I shall. . .'; see Chapter 5.5).

4. Value and signification

Chapters II and III of the second part of the CGL establish the theoretical necessity of value, but it is in Chapter IV – often regarded as the book's finest – that it is developed, again starting from the remark that in themselves the domains of thought and sound are confused and shapeless, and only assume form in the linguistic division which segments these continua.

Langue, then, is a system which organizes terms on the basis of their relations. Between them these terms share the totality of the material for signifying, thereby creating values through which signification is instituted. Linguistic entities are values because they are the terms of a system.

But signification was already at issue in the definition of the sign, in which the signified is the signifying counterpart of the signifier. So what is the relation between signified, signification and value?

Signification emerges from the relationship between signifier and signified, 'when we look upon the word as independent and self-contained' (p. 114). Saussure represents this in a diagram which we have already encountered.

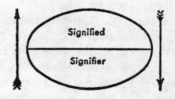

But the principle of difference has served to establish that the sign is 'the counterpart of the other signs of language [*langue*]'. By means of value Saussure contests a conception of *langue* wherein the sign is a self-enclosed unit. The interdependence of signs is represented by another diagram:

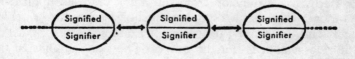

55

where the horizontal arrows represent the relations between the signs, the inauguration of value.

'Language [*langue*] is a system of interdependent terms in which the value of each term results solely from the simultaneous presence of the others' (p. 114). This can be illustrated by comparing the English *sheep* and the French *mouton*. They have the same meaning – but not the same value. *Sheep* is different from *mutton*, which French also translates by *mouton*. In order to approximate to the value of *mouton*, it is necessary to show that it is not *bélier* ('ram'), *agneau* ('lamb'), *brebis* ('ewe'), *cheval* ('horse'). . . The value of *sheep* is constituted by the same oppositions, with the added proviso that it is not *mutton*. The meaning of each term is circumscribed by these oppositions.

Difference is not a secondary characteristic of a unit; it is constitutive of this unit. The meaning of unit *a* is not established by considering its positive qualities, but by abstracting it from them, so that it is merely *not-b*, *not-c*, etc.

At the same time Saussure recalls the dual character of any value as traditionally and generally defined: a value is generated by the relation between two dissimilar things, which can be exchanged, and two similar things, which can be compared. This definition is supported by a comparison with a monetary currency. Dissimilar things: a coin and whatever may be bought with it. Similar things: one coin compared with the other coins in the currency. We can now see how there might be two intersecting approaches to signification. The sign involves two completely different things – the idea and the sound. When two similar things are compared (a sign with another sign), the relation gives rise to a value. Signified and value must overlap in signification.

Value is what makes signification possible, both on the lexical and the grammatical levels. On the lexical level, it is easy to see that significations are the product of reciprocal limitations. Moreover, there is no such thing as an absolute synonym; each term derives its extension from the limits imposed upon it by the others. Thus each of the three quasi-synonyms *redouter*, *craindre* and *avoir peur* ('to fear'), for example, is distinguished by the fact that it is not the others. The same applies to the grammatical level, where Saussure offers the example of the plural, which does not have the same value in French – where it is only opposed to the singular – and in Greek, whose morphological system includes the dual (referring to two persons or things). Similarly, the value of a French imperfect and that of a German preterite are not the same – although their signification may be – in so far as French opposes to it a *passé simple* unknown in German; the value of French and English passives is not identical; etc.

On both the grammatical and the lexical levels, value, and hence signification, are the result of the reciprocal limitation of signs by one another: 'When you add a sign to the language, you proportionately reduce the signification of the other signs. By the same token, if by some miracle a mere two signs had been selected at the outset, all the significations would be shared between them. One would stand for half the objects, the other for the other half' (Course II).

Value derives from the arbitrary nature of the sign, and '*Arbitrary* and *differential* are two correlative qualities' (p. 118). But this relation is somewhat obscured in the CGL by an error on the part of the editors, who write: 'values remain entirely relative, and that is why the bond between the sound and the idea is radically arbitrary' (p. 113). The sources read: 'Values remain entirely relative because the bond is entirely arbitrary' (CLG, p. 464). The effect of the editorial alteration is to present the cause as the consequence.

This is not the only occasion on which the presentation of the CGL makes it more difficult to understand. The same may be said of the diagram, in which the inter-relation of the signs (represented by horizontal arrows) seems to be a secondary effect, involving previously constituted signs. The constitutive role of this inter-relation is thereby obscured. However, value does serve to oppose language as nomenclature: 'Instead of pre-existing ideas then, we find ... *values* emanating from the system. When they are said to correspond to concepts, it is understood that the concepts are purely differential and defined not by their positive content but negatively by their relations with the other terms of the system' (p. 117).

Value, then, is determinant for signification. But is signification solely deducible from value? Some additional comments are called for here.

To begin with, value is a potentiality of *langue*, signification a realization of *parole* (see Chapter 5). Next, value and signification do not completely coincide, since there is a 'surplus of value' which a term may acquire from its proximity to another term that originally had no signification in common with it: the sense of *décrépit* (as in *un vieillard décrépit* 'a decrepit old man') is enriched by its confusion with *décrépi* (as in *un mur décrépi* 'a wall from which mortar is falling'). We shall see the connection between this idea and the associations which constitute a term in Chapter 6.

However, close examination of a sentence on p. 114 of the CGL indicates that we may not simply conclude that value dominates signification: 'From a conceptual viewpoint, value is doubtless one element in signification, and it is difficult to see how signification can be dependent upon value and still be distinct from it.' This contains two apparently contradictory assertions:
– value is one element in signification;
– signification is dependent upon value.

Whilst the analysis offered here satisfies the second point, it precludes the first. To reconcile them, we may advance the following hypothesis: with the concept of value Saussure is describing the linguistic component of signification. This leaves a whole side of things which also plays a role in the constitution of meaning, but which concerns everything excluded by the founding dichotomies (see Chapter 5) and therefore remains outside the scope of linguistics.

It should be noted that Saussure never uses the term *semantics*, which from the end of the nineteenth century designated the discipline concerned with the organization of meaning in *langue*. Since he was on the point of succeeding Bréal, the word's inventor, in his chair at the Collège de France in Paris in 1891, Saussure can hardly have been unaware of it. Was it due to his lack of interest in the discipline as then constituted? Diffidence in face of the problems of interpretation? Whatever the reason, I propose to interpret it as an effect of Saussure's philosophical position on *langue*: *langue* in its entirety is not the preserve of the linguist (see Chapter 5); other disciplines have a legitimate interest in it.

Value represents Saussure's most radical innovation in linguistics, the most irreducible to all his antecedents and contemporaries. Its essential characteristic lies in the absence of material identity, or rather, the contingent aspect of material identity: a sign, a signifier or a signified can vary so long as they do not risk becoming confused with others. A unit is only limited by the resistance of other units (in other words, it is a negative limitation). The principle of the unity of *langue* thus established will have major consequences for linguistic research. Since languages function in relation to themselves, priority may be accorded to operations of commutation and comparison on the basis of membership of the same system. The CGL reiterates it, and it is one of Saussure's central theses: '*language* [*langue*] *is a form and not a substance*' (pp. 122, 113). A system of values is not formed from phonic-acoustic and semantic materials (two substances, two shapeless masses which do not contain the principles of their own organization), but creates linguistic figures out of substances by endowing them with form.

Further Reading

CGL:
Part One, chapter III
Part Two, chapters I, II, III, IV

Jean-Louis Chiss, 'Synchronie/diachronie: méthodologie et théorie en linguistique', *Langages* 49, 1978.
Oswald Ducrot, 'Le Structuralisme en linguistique', *Qu'est-ce que le structuralisme?*, Seuil, Paris 1968.
Rudolf Engler, *Lexique de la terminologie saussurienne*, Spectrum, Utrecht and Anvers 1968.
Claudine Normand, 'Propositions et notes en vue d'une lecture de F. de Saussure', *La Pensée* 154, 1970.

5

The Object

Extract from the CGL, Introduction, Chapter III

Through the functioning of the receptive and co-ordinating facul-
ties, impressions that are perceptibly the same for all are made
on the minds of speakers. How can that social product be pictured
in such a way that language [*langue*] will stand apart from everything else? If we could embrace the sum of word-images stored
in the minds of all individuals, we could identify the social bond
that constitutes language [*langue*]. It is a storehouse filled by the
members of a given community through their active use of
speaking [*parole*], a grammatical system that has a potential existence in each brain, or, more specifically, in the brains of a
group of individuals. For language [*langue*] is not complete in any
speaker; it exists perfectly only within a collectivity.

In separating language [*langue*] from speaking [*parole*] we are
at the same time separating: (1) what is social from what is
individual; and (2) what is essential from what is accessory and
more or less accidental.

Language [*langue*] is not a function of the speaker; it is a
product that is passively assimilated by the individual. It never
requires premeditation, and reflection enters in only for the
purpose of classification, which we shall take up later (pp. 122ff.).

Speaking [*parole*], on the contrary, is an individual act. It is
wilful and intellectual. Within the act, we should distinguish
between: (1) the combinations by which the speaker uses the
language code for expressing his own thought; and (2) the psych-
ophysical mechanism that allows him to exteriorize those
combinations.

Note that I have defined things rather than words; these definitions are not endangered by certain ambiguous words that do not have identical meanings in different languages. For instance, German *Sprache* means both 'language' and 'speech'; *Rede* almost corresponds to 'speaking' but adds the special connotation of 'discourse.' Latin *sermo* designates both 'speech' and 'speaking,' while *lingua* means 'language,' etc. No word corresponds exactly to any of the notions specified above; that is why all definitions of words are made in vain; starting from words in defining things is a bad procedure.

To summarize, these are the characteristics of language [*langue*]:

1) Language [*langue*] is a well-defined object in the heterogeneous mass of speech facts. It can be localized in the limited segment of the speaking-circuit where an auditory image becomes associated with a concept. It is the social side of speech, outside the individual who can never create nor modify it by himself; it exists only by virtue of a sort of contract signed by the members of a community. Moreover, the individual must always serve an apprenticeship in order to learn the functioning of language; a child assimilates it only gradually. It is such a distinct thing that a man deprived of the use of speaking [*parole*] retains it provided that he understands the vocal signs that he hears.

2) Language [*langue*], unlike speaking [*parole*], is something that we can study separately. Although we no longer speak dead languages, we are certainly capable of assimilating their linguistic systems. We can dispense with the other elements of speech; indeed, the science of language is possible only if the other elements are excluded.

3) Whereas speech [*langage*] is heterogeneous, language [*langue*], as defined, is homogeneous. It is a system of signs in which the only essential thing is the union of meanings and sound-images, and in which both parts of the sign are psychological.

4) Language [*langue*] is concrete, no less so than speaking [*parole*]; and this is a help in our study of it. Linguistic signs, though basically psychological, are not abstractions; associations which bear the stamp of collective approval – and which added together constitute language – are realities that have their seat in the brain. Besides, linguistic signs are tangible; it is possible to

61

reduce them to conventional written symbols, whereas it would be impossible to provide detailed photographs of acts of speaking [*actes de parole*]; the pronunciation of even the smallest word represents an infinite number of muscular movements that could be identified and put into graphic form only with great difficulty. In language [*langue*], on the contrary, there is only the sound-image, and the latter can be translated into a fixed visual image. For if we disregard the vast number of movements necessary for the realization of sound-images in speaking, we see that each sound-image is nothing more than the sum of a limited number of elements or phonemes that can in turn be called up by a corresponding number of written symbols (see pp. 61 ff.). The very possibility of putting the things that relate to language [*langue*] into graphic form allows dictionaries and grammars to represent it accurately, for language [*langue*] is a storehouse of sound-images, and writing is the tangible form of those images.

Course in General Linguistics, Introduction, Chapter III, pp. 13–15

It may seem strange to be examining the object and status of a discipline practised as if it were unproblematic only at this late stage. And indeed in the CGL the problem of the object and the definition of *langue* and *parole* occurs much earlier, in the Introduction. Yet the sources reveal that for Saussure a discussion of these issues presupposed the definition of other concepts and investigation of the ideas examined in the two preceding chapters. So the plan of the CGL notwithstanding, and at the risk of interrupting a coherent discussion of *system* and *mechanism*, it seems preferable to consider them here.

One of the tasks Saussurian linguistics assigns itself is a consideration of its object and the framework in which it is inscribed. Judging from the history of linguistics, this framework is not self-evident. For linguistics has successively or simultaneously proposed mergers with various disciplines: logical philosophy (Aristotle or Port-Royal), the natural sciences (Schleicher in the nineteenth century), history (the comparatists), psychology (Wundt or Bally at the end of the nineteenth century). Obviously, these are only highly schematic indications;

the links between linguistics, philosophy, history, rhetoric and logic, etc., have always been complex.

In order to establish his own position, in which linguistics becomes a component part of semiology because it is obliged to examine the determination of its object, Saussure seeks to extricate it from the philosophical and historical viewpoints with which it was frequently bound up at the beginning of the century. The philosophers are criticized for neglecting evolution, the historians for forgetting the existence of language-states. 'Studies of language [*langue*] by non-linguists do not tackle the subject in its essentials' (Course II). Saussure makes the definition of the essential – *langue* as a system of signs – his priority.

1. 'No object anterior to analysis'

This phrase from a note of Saussure's (SM, p. 47) poses the problem of the object of linguistics, which Saussure expounds starting from the distinction between the *subject-matter* (the totality of linguistic phenomena) and the *object* (the region of linguistic facts adopted by the linguist). The subject-matter comprises the totality of linguistic facts, but the object of linguistics is *langue* as formal system.

Hence 'object' must be taken in the strong sense. It is not something inscribed in the reality of linguistic facts, but the organizing principle of a discipline – a manner of ordering facts: 'it is the viewpoint that creates the object' (p. 8). This position recognizes the legitimacy of other, non-linguistic viewpoints on language.[1]

Assigning an object to linguistics, necessitates first and foremost a distinction between *langue* and *langage*. *Langage* is simultaneously faculty and institution: the faculty of language [*langage*], peculiar to human beings, remains unrealized so long as it does not crystallize in the institution that is *langue*: 'Nature produces man organized for articulated language [*langage*], but without articulated language. Language [*langue*] is a social fact' (SM, p. 148). Such expressions as *the French language, the German language*, etc., capture this first distinction.

Language is always characterized by a notional duality; it is simultaneously faculty and institution, production and reception, phonic substance and thought, individual act and social fact, system and evolution. In short, it possesses an 'irritating duplicity which makes it impossible to pin down' (EC, 1485F). Saussure's conceptual dichotomies register this duality, going beyond a mere recognition of antinomies, and are a way of situating oneself in the debates which it has provoked.

The definition of *langue* is established through a number of filters. The first is a distinction between internal and external elements: 'My definition of language [*langue*] presupposes the exclusion of everything that is outside its organism or system' (p. 20). This involves the elimination of all the external causes and determinations that may act upon language: ethnological, political, institutional and geographical facts are all factors that 'do not actually affect the inner organism of an idiom' (p. 21). Saussure illustrates the distinction by his first comparison with chess: the origin of the game and the material or form of the pieces are external; only those aspects pertaining to the actual rules of the game are internal.

Linguistics' 'relations with other sciences' – ethnography, prehistory, anthropology, sociology, social psychology, but also physiology and philology – 'from which [it] must be carefully distinguished' (p. 6), are stated in accordance with the same principle and for the same reasons.

The strongest argument in favour of a distinction between internal and external linguistics stresses the different methods characteristic of them. Whereas external linguistics facilitates the accumulation of facts, internal linguistics, for which 'language [*langue*] is a system that has its own arrangement' (p. 22), is concerned with 'everything that changes the system in any way' (p. 23). Here Saussurian linguistics is opposed to its contemporaries: in an era predominantly concerned with external linguistics, it was to be internal.

In Chapter 3 we saw how the very definition of the sign as bond between signifier and signified, and the arbitrariness attributed to it, clarify two further dichotomies through exclusion:

– *Langue* and reality: any reference to the domain of things

64

is eliminated from the object of linguistics, defined as a domain of signs.

– *Langue* and thought: 'The characteristic role of language [*langue*] with respect to thought is not to create a material phonic means for expressing ideas but to serve as a link between thought and sound, under conditions that of necessity bring about the reciprocal delimitations of units' (p. 112). Thus Saussure postulates that there is no thought that exists independently of *langue*. The signified is not anterior to the signifier.

These dichotomies are marginal to the essential task – the definition of *langue*, object of linguistics – which is assured by the two conceptual couples *langue/parole* and synchrony/diachrony.

Here we shall refer to the synchrony/diachrony distinction – already defined in Chapter 4 – only in order to illustrate the interpretative problems to which the dichotomies lead. Essentially three kinds of reading can be found in commentaries:

– A naive reading, in which synchrony and diachrony are two aspects of one and the same object. As De Mauro remarks ironically: 'The *langue*-object has a synchrony and a diachrony just as M. Durand has a hat and a pair of gloves' (CLG, p. 452).

– A methodological reading, which reduces the opposition to two different but complementary perspectives on an object whose existence is otherwise obvious – whence the possibility of two types of linguistics, the synchronic and the diachronic.

– A theoretical reading which, regardless of the properties displayed by the object or of the need for a method, registers a distinction that establishes the preconditions for linguistics as a science. A method is deducible, but only from the fact of this theoretical distinction.

The opposition between *langue* and *parole*, on which we shall now concentrate, distinguishing between what pertains to the system of *langue* and what comes under the metamorphoses of its employment, redoubles the dichotomy between synchrony and diachrony; 'the only real object of linguistics is the normal, regular life of an existing idiom' (p. 72) – *langue* in synchrony.

2. *Langue*, institution and system

The basic dichotomy between *langue* and *parole* establishes *langue* as a principle of classification of the heterogeneous facts that make up language.

'Langue' appears for the first time in a circular argument: '*from the very outset we must put both feet on the ground of language* [langue] *and use [it] as the norm of all other manifestations of speech* [langage]' (p. 9). The CGL ends on the same note: '*the true and unique object of linguistics is language* [langue] *studied in and for itself*' (p. 232). These definitions should not be taken as a veto, but as an epistemological *prise de position*. Moreover, it should be noted that the most radical formulations derive from the editors – for example, the reference to '. . . several sciences . . . which are [utterly] distinct from linguistics' (p. 9). Saussure's sole concern was to orientate linguistic research, not to accredit the linguist with the only true outlook on language.

Langue is primarily defined by a series of oppositions between it and *parole*:

Langue	Parole
Social	Individual
Essential	Incidental
Passively registered	Act of will and intelligence
Psychological	Psycho-physical
Sum of imprints in each brain	Sum of what people say
Collective model	Non-collective

A certain heterogeneity is evident here, dictating closer examination of these definitions.

In the exposition of the *langue/parole* dichotomy, two networks of definitions are intertwined in the same passages. On the one hand, *langue* is a social institution – for example: 'It is both a social product of the faculty of speech [*langage*] and a collection of necessary conventions' (p. 9). On the other, *langue* is a system of signs – for example: 'Language [*langue*] . . . is a self-contained whole and a principle of classification' (p. 9) or 'a system that has its own arrangement' (p. 22).

This inevitably poses the question of what connection exists between the two kinds of definition (semiological and sociological) – all the more so since the text is not explicit on this point. Are they complementary? Or contradictory?

In defence of their compatibility, two lines of argument have been proposed, making the sociological follow from the semiological or vice versa: (1) The sociological follows from the semiological. Because *langue* is a system of values it is resistant to individual innovations and hence can function as a social institution; (2) The semiological follows from the sociological. Arbitrariness is radical in so far as it derives from the social nature of language, and hence *langue* is a system.

Whatever conceptual link may be reconstructed between these two types of definition, it remains to consider their linguistic utility. In this respect they are indeed contradictory. With the sociological definition, Saussure is on common ground with the majority of his contemporaries; whereas the semiological definition advances an original position – the very birth of modern linguistics. It permits the emergence of the abstract study of *langue* – something expressed in the radical last sentence of the CGL: '*the true and unique object of linguistics is language* [langue] *studied in and for itself*' (p. 232).

3. 'To show the linguist what he is doing'

If Saussure's letter of 1894 to Meillet is to be believed (see p. 19), 'to show the linguist what he is doing' is all the more indispensable given that the object of linguistics only exists in a viewpoint. The linguist must be made aware of the nature of his activity when he does what he is doing.

The raw material confronting the linguist belongs to the order of *parole*. Access to *langue* is not the result of direct observation, since it is a kind of 'thread', closely woven and abstract, which endows the substance that is *parole* with form. Access to *langue* may only be obtained via *parole*.

Concrete raw material/abstract net: the *langue/parole* opposition thus also contains an opposition between *concrete* (*parole*) and *abstract* (*langue*). But these terms are of modern provenance.

One senses a reluctance on Saussure's part to use the word 'abstract'. A possible explanation for its quasi-absence (it is only found in a negative context) is that in an era dominated by Kantian epistemology, Saussure considered it pejorative. Although now considered one of the initiators of access to the abstract in the twentieth century, paradoxically, he hesitated to use the term, inducing formulations whose caution renders them maladroit. Examples would be the statement that 'although purely spiritual, these signs are not abstractions' (EC, 263 B) or the characterization of *langue* as 'psychological'. *Psychological* and *spiritual* are both approximations to an *abstract* which dare not speak its name.

The fact that the linguist reaches *langue* via *parole* justifies the order of exposition adopted by Saussure in the third course, which is quite different from the CGL's. It has frequently been remarked that the introduction of the *langue/parole* opposition among the first concepts of the CGL make it particularly difficult to grasp – so much so that it has been described as 'hanging in the air'. Its preliminary position was doubtless understood by the editors as according with Saussure's statement in an interview in which he characterizes the distinction between *langue* and *parole* as the 'first truth' of his system (see p. 20). But how is this truth arrived at? Clearly, the evidence is insufficient. From the first course to the third Saussure graduated towards a presentation which commences with examination of the concrete – *parole* – whose manifest variation provokes the crucial question of identity: how can elements which do or may differ radically come to have identity for speaking subjects? What substantiates judgements of identity?

We saw in Chapter 4 that the answer to this question involves the postulation of the concept of value, which makes it possible to treat identity as a relational phenomenon. Simultaneously, this concept supplies the best possible theoretical basis for the difference between *langue* and *parole*: identity, and hence difference, which is not founded on a physical or semantic justification, is the sole guarantee of the reality of signification. *Langue* is a linguistic knowledge primarily displayed in judgements of identity and difference.

The CGL's order of exposition, which features *langue/parole* from the outset, is therefore paradoxical. The significance of the pair comes into sharper focus when the order of Saussure's third course is restored: first, an examination of diachronic and synchronic identities; next, the arbitrary nature of the sign which, through value, makes it possible to arrive at *langue* as form; and only then the *langue/parole* opposition.

4. *Langue*, from memory to constraint

The semiological definition of *langue* has two apparently irreducible features: the system as creative functioning or as product of memory. Given its implications for the role of syntax in a theory of *langue*, we shall pause over this. From the perspective of memory, the *langue/parole* opposition can be expressed as follows:

$$langue = \text{passivity} = \text{memory}$$
$$parole = \text{activity} = \text{creation}$$

In effect, *langue* 'is passively assimilated by the individual' (p. 14). It involves neither premeditation nor reflection, whereas *parole* is 'an individual act . . . wilful and intellectual' (p. 14). But just as semiological and sociological perspectives were intertwined, the mnemonic definitions are intermixed with others. Thus, in the following sentence, semiology and memory: *langue* 'is a storehouse filled by the members of a given community through their active use of speaking [*parole*], a grammatical system that has a potential existence in each brain' (pp. 13–14). *Storehouse* and *system* perform the same function in the sentence. But are they equivalent? There would appear to be a patent contradiction between 'storehouse', which cannot but suggest a fixed and static conception, and what is implied by 'system', which posits the existence of a mechanism observable only in its effects (whence the importance of 'potential').

One finds this same admixture throughout the exposition of *langue*; such static terms as 'impression' (p. 13) and 'storehouse' (p. 15) figure in passages developing the system's creative possibilities. In the context in which it appears, 'dictionary' is to be understood in the same way ('almost like a dictionary of which identical copies have been distributed to each individual' (p. 19) – a definition which mixes mnemonic and sociological definitions. The same intersection is again present in the exposition of associative and syntagmatic relations (see Chapter 6). Whilst the former are characterized as 'a potential mnemonic series' (p. 123), they serve to expound the functioning of *langue* (pp. 127ff.). Accordingly, it is vital that we go beyond the static implications of Saussure's evocation of the role of memory in the functioning of *langue*, and study the relations between the respective roles allotted to memory and creativity.

Here a real problem arises: in the final analysis, the mnemonic definition has the effect of allocating all activity to *parole*; *langue* is mere assimilation and submission, involving only a meagre classificatory activity by way of initiative ('there is never any premeditation, nor even meditation, reflection on the forms, outside of the act, the occasion of *parole*, save for an unconscious, uncreative activity: classification' (SM, p. 58).

This derives from the attribution of the individual aspect solely to *parole*. We should note Saussure's hesitation here, for the sources indicate that *langue* was initially divided into an individual aspect and a collective aspect (SM, p. 145). But in the CGL the faculty of creation, and hence the freedom enjoyed by the speaking subject, is attributed solely to *parole*. Conversely, facts pertaining to *langue* leave no room for creativity. In sum, the system is identified with constraint.

The conception of the system as constraint, and the allocation of creation to *parole*, pose numerous questions for the constitution of a syntax. If grammar must account for the fact that every new sentence is an original combination, making a regulated use of creativity, syntax cannot be defined either as constraint or product of freedom, but has to be seen as a combination of the two.

Do the mnemonic aspects of Saussure's definition of *langue* preclude syntax? Do they reveal that it was not a crucial theoretical problem for him? We must now examine what form a Saussurian syntax might take.

5. The status of the sentence: what space for syntax?

The *langue/parole* opposition has provoked numerous discussions among linguists. We are going to focus on Chomsky's criticisms, since they concern the place of syntax.

On several occasions Chomsky instances his debt to Saussure, whose *langue/parole* opposition he basically adopts in his own distinction between competence and performance. But only 'basically', for his critique centres on the status accorded to the sentence: 'it is necessary to reject his concept of *langue* as merely a systematic inventory of items'.[2] This raises several questions. Is it true that for Saussure *langue* is merely an 'inventory of items'? Does the Saussurian conception of *langue* preclude any creative syntax?

Let us begin with 'items', so as to refute the interpretation of 'sign' exclusively as 'word'. To be sure, 'sign' appears to refer above all to the lexical term. Yet it is clear both that it is often to be understood as inferior to the word (the morpheme, minimal unit of signification) and that nothing prevents it being extended beyond the word ('We do not communicate through isolated signs but rather through groups of signs, through organized masses that are themselves signs' – p. 128). Moreover, the hesitation between *word* and *item* must be underlined; its implications are set out in a note from the sources: 'As soon as we say "term" rather than "word", the idea of system is evoked' (SM, p. 90; the formal meaning of *term* must be borne in mind here).

The phrase 'inventory of items' is equally open to question. In Chapter 4 we saw that the notion of element had to be constructed; hence the elements cannot be the object of an inventory. In literal terms, then, Chomsky's critique is polemical and inapposite.

Nevertheless, the status of the *syntagm* (as we shall see in Chapter 6, in Saussure the word does not have its modern meaning) and of the *sentence* is undoubtedly a tricky subject for Saussure. His discomfort is evident whenever the issue of the sentence arises: 'But to what extent does the sentence belong to language [*langue*]... .? If it belongs to speaking [*parole*], the sentence cannot pass for [*ne saurait passer pour*] the linguistic unit' (p. 106). Saussure switches from the interrogative to the conditional. Further on, we find an assertion containing an opposition: 'The sentence is the ideal type of syntagm. But it belongs to speaking [*parole*], not to language [*langue*]' (p. 124). Albeit not without some hesitation, the CGL thus resolves the problem by placing the sentence on the side of *parole*.

However, the sources once again reveal a more nuanced attitude to the relations between the functioning of *langue* and creativity: 'In sum, it is only in *syntax* that there appears a wavering between what is fixed by *langue* and what is left to individual freedom' (SM, p. 169).

Undoubtedly, Saussure did not make all the use of syntax he might have. Even so, and over and above explicit statements, several passages in the CGL indicate that judgement of the relationship between functioning of *langue* and creativity established by Saussure can be qualified:

– The creation of a word like *indécorable* on the model of existing forms illustrates the role of 'regular forms' in *langue* (p. 125):

When a word like *indécorable* arises in speaking [*parole*] (see pp. 167ff.), its appearance supposes a fixed type, and this type is in turn possible only through remembrance of a sufficient number of similar words belonging to language [*langue*] (*impardonable* 'unpardonable', *intolérable* 'intolerable', *infatigable* 'indefatigable', etc.). Exactly the same is true of sentences and groups of words built upon regular patterns. Combinations like *la terre tourne* 'the world turns', *que vous dit-il?* 'what does he say to you?', etc. correspond to general types that are in turn supported in the language by concrete remembrance.

But we must realize that in the syntagm there is no clear-cut boundary between the language [*langue*] fact, which is a sign of collective usage, and the fact that belongs to speaking [*parole*] and depends on individual freedom.

Certainly, such a formation will first of all appear in *parole* – but only in so far as it obeys a determinate schema. And the presence of the problematic of memory is mitigated by a genuine anxiety about the role of creativity.

– The use of any word simultaneously brings into play associative and syntagmatic relations. A word like *marchons* ['(let's) walk!'), supposing as it does a series of exclusions (it is not *chantons* '(let's) sing!', nor *marchez* '(you) walk!'], contains in embryo a syntax of the distributional type: 'the idea evokes not a form but a whole latent system that makes possible the oppositions necessary for the formation of the sign' (p. 130). Since it is immediately specified that 'this principle applies to even the most complex types of syntagms and sentences', it can be seen that *sign* and *sentence* are not mutually exclusive and there is no boundary between them.

– In his analysis of the component parts of a grammar, Saussure demonstrates that the division between syntax and lexicology (and *a fortiori* morphology) is not a natural one, and that grammar could perfectly well do without it: 'There is basically no distinction between any word that is not a simple, irreducible unit and a phrase, which is a syntactical fact. The arrangement of the subunits of the word obeys the same fundamental principles as the arrangement of groups of words in phrases' (p. 136).

– The idea that 'analogy is grammatical. It supposes awareness and understanding of a relation between forms' (p. 165). Creation initially occurs in *parole*, but it 'must be preceded by an unconscious comparison of the materials deposited in the storehouse of language [*langue*], where productive forms are arranged according to their syntagmatic and associative relations'. Once again, the text is contradictory: 'storehouse' and 'arrange' (memory) on the one hand, 'productive forms' and reference to the unconscious functioning of the relations (creativity) on the other. A little further on comes the idea that existing forms are able to persist because they are continually renewed analogically: synchronic functioning and creation come under the same mechanism.

These four points, which open the way to a creative Saussurian syntax, merit fuller discussion – something undertaken in Chapter 6.

Thus Saussure comes very close to what Chomsky formulates explicitly. Chomsky counterposes a 'rule-governed creativity' (creation of new forms – including sentences – within the schemas supplied by grammar) to a 'creativity changing the rules' (errors of every kind, lapsus, extra-grammatical creations). This distinction makes it possible to resolve the apparent contradiction between freedom and constraint in *langue*, for the sentence can be conceived as a creativity that respects constraining principles.

Hence a syntax is possible in Saussure, as long as it is conceived in the same way as the rest of *langue*: 'in the last analysis what is commonly referred to as a "grammatical fact" fits the definition of the unit, for it always expresses an opposition of terms' (p. 121). This reminds us that everything hangs together in *langue*, that the 'normal, regular life of an existing idiom' is *langue* in synchrony, wherein everything is analysed according to the interplay of identities and differences.

Further Reading

CGL:
Introduction, Chapters II, III, IV and V
Part Two

Noam Chomsky, *Current Issues in Linguistic Theory*, Mouton, The Hague 1964.
——, *Aspects of the Theory of Syntax*, MIT Press, Cambridge (Mass.) 1965.
Oswald Ducrot and Tzvetan Todorov, *Encyclopedic Dictionary of the Sciences of Language*, Basil Blackwell, Oxford 1981 (article on Language and Speech).
Claudine Normand, 'Langue/parole: constitution et enjeu d'une opposition', *Langages* 49, 1978.
Denis Slakta, 'Esquisse d'une théorie lexico-sémantique: pour une analyse d'un texte politique', *Langages* 23, 1971.

6

The Mechanism

Extract from the CGL, Part Two, Chapter VIII

Role of Abstract Entities in Grammar

One important subject, not yet touched upon, points up this very necessity of examining every grammatical question from the two viewpoints specified in Chapter VII: abstract entities in grammar. Let us consider them first associatively.

To associate two forms is not only to feel that they have something in common but also to single out the nature of the relations that govern associations. For instance, speakers are aware that the relation between *enseigner* and *enseignement* or *juger* and *jugement* is not the same as the relation between *enseignement* and *jugement* 'judgment' (see p. 125). This is how the system of associations is tied to the system of grammar. We can say that the sum of the conscious and methodical classifications made by the grammarian who studies a language-state without bringing in history must coincide with the associations, conscious or not, that are set up in speaking [*parole*]. These associations fix word-families, inflectional paradigms, and formative elements (radicals, suffixes, inflectional endings, etc.) in our minds (see pp. 185 ff.).

But does association single out only material elements? No, of course not. We have already seen that it brings together words that are related only through meaning (cf. *enseignement, apprentissage, éducation*, etc.). The same must apply in grammar. Take the three Latin genitive forms *domin-ī, rēg-is, ros-ārum*. The sounds of the three endings offer no basis for association, yet the endings are connected by the feeling that they have a common

75

value which prescribes an identical function. This suffices to create the association in the absence of any material support, and the notion of the genitive in this way takes its place in the language. Through a similar procedure, the inflectional endings -*us*, -*ī*, -*ō*, etc (in *dominus, dominī, dominō*, etc.) are linked together in the mind and are the basis for the more general notions of case and case endings. Associations of the same class, but larger still, combine all substantives, adjectives, etc. and fix the notion of parts of speech.

All these things exist in language [*langue*], but as *abstract entities*; their study is difficult because we never know exactly whether or not the awareness of speakers goes as far as the analyses of the grammarian. But the important thing is that *abstract entities are always based, in the last analysis, on concrete entities*. No grammatical abstraction is possible without a series of material elements as a basis, and in the end we must always come back to these elements.

Now we turn to the syntagmatic viewpoint. The value of a cluster is often linked to the order of its elements. In analyzing a syntagm, the speaker does not restrict himself to singling out its parts; he observes a certain order of succession among them. The meaning of English *pain-ful* or Latin *signi-fer* depends on the respective positions of their subunits: we cannot say *ful-pain* or *fer-signum*. A value may have no relations with a concrete element (like -*ful* or -*fer*) and result solely from the arrangement of the terms; for instance, the different significations of the two clusters in French *je dois* 'I must' and *dois-je?* 'must I?' are due only to word order.

Course in General Linguistics, Part Two, Chapter VIII, pp. 137–38

We have established that *langue* is form and not substance, that the definition of term is exclusively a matter for the order of *langue* itself, and therefore of relations of identity and difference between them in a system of pure values. Linguistics is therefore the interrelation of signs ('All phenomena are relations between relations', EC, 1968 – a statement found in all the student notebooks). It remains to describe the mechanism of language [*langue*], by studying the nature of the relations between the elements, both in the system and in its realization, through the linearity of the spoken chain, in discourse.

1. The paradox of the concrete unit

We have already seen that Saussure contests the linguistics of his era, especially in his insistence that the unit with which linguistics works is not an obvious datum: 'At first glance *langue* strikes us as not presenting graspable concrete units – though this doesn't mean we can reject the idea that they must exist in the first place' (EC, 1753E). Only if he lets himself be blinded by the evidence as it functions for speaking subjects can the linguist fail to pose the crucial question: whence derives the knowledge that subjects dispose of units? What is it based upon?

Saussure's procedure is to argue from an immediate reality: 'Being unable to seize the concrete entities or units of language [*langue*] directly, we shall work with words. While the word does not conform exactly to the definition of the linguistic unit . . ., it at least bears a rough resemblance to the unit and has the advantage of being concrete' (pp. 113–14). A segmental definition of the word (making it a section of the spoken chain associating a signifier and a signified) is quickly seen to be inadequate; *cheval* and *chevaux* ('horses'), *dans* without elision and *dans* with elision would be two different words, whereas for speakers they are one and the same.

Over and above any simple delimitation in the signifier, the concrete unit is therefore whatever is significant to any degree for speaking subjects, as a result of a judgement of identity. The same word can be recognized in *cheval* and *chevaux* only by relegating the material expression to a subordinate level. Objectively different segments can be representatives of the same unit because *langue* is form and not substance.

How are the units established? Rather than 'cutting up the chain with scissors', it must be assumed that there is a complex mechanism which ensures the functioning of the combinations that are words, both in their systemic potential and linear realization. Since everything available for understanding is manifest in the linearity of the chain (the only thing to which we have access), the functioning of this mechanism may be conceived as the projection onto the linear of everything in play in the system. Thus a distinction must be made (remaining on the level of *langue*) between the potential system and the possibilities

77

of arrangement into sequences – a stage of *langue* that is not to be confused with effective realization, which pertains to *parole*.

Thus between *parole* – the only thing open to observation – and *langue* – object of linguistic reflection – there is the profundity of the functioning of the mechanism, assured by two spheres: the syntagmatic (order of linearity) and the associative (order of the system).

2. Chain of discourse and constellation

'Relations and differences between linguistic terms fall into two distinct groups, each of which generates a certain class of values' (p. 123).

The first type of relations is as follows. In the linear chain, the elements maintain relations of contiguity. A unit cannot be combined with just any unit (e.g., an adjective can be combined with a noun, but not with a verb). Moreover, word-order is not unimportant. Thus in French – a language in which word-order plays a particularly important role – *Pierre aime Marie* ('Peter loves Marie') does not mean the same as *Marie aime Pierre*. Saussure calls these linear relations, *in praesentia*, syntagmatic.

In the CGL, contrary to its subsequent use in linguistics, the term 'syntagm' applies to any linguistic sequence, from the complex word to the sentence, as soon as it is open to analysis. Without exception, syntagmatic organization exhibits a solidarity between the elements: the largest elements are constituted from the smallest, in a bond of reciprocal solidarity. The rare cases of independent units do not represent a serious objection to this principle, since we speak via groups of signs. 'In language [*langue*] everything boils down to differences *but also to groupings* (p. 128; my emphasis). So syntagmatic organization is decisive.

Given that the same principle of solidarity applies to the sentence, the problem of the latter's status resurfaces. We have seen that the sentence was classified as *parole*. But the syntagm (the possibility of syntagmatic combination) undoubtedly pertains to *langue*, because there exist 'idiomatic twists ... furnished by tradition' (e.g., *allons donc!* 'nonsense!', *forcer la main à quelqu'un* 'force someone's hand', etc.), but above all because of 'the syntagmatic types that are built upon regular forms' (e.g., *indécorable*) (pp. 124–25). The analysis of *indécorable* being immediately extended to 'sentences and groups of words built upon regular patterns', two apparently contradictory propositions must be rendered compatible:

– the sentence pertains to *parole*;

– the syntagm, and the particular case of the sentence, come under the analysability of the system, hence *langue*.

Nothing in the CGL explicitly serves to resolve this problem. An interpretation may nevertheless be proposed which is not in contradiction with it. The two sentences cited (*La terre tourne* and *Que vous dit-il?*), both of them stereotyped in their way, give us reason to think that for Saussure the difficulty lies in the quota of constraint and freedom attributed to *langue* and *parole*. Now, the sentence is simultaneously constraint (it activates the rules of *langue*) and creativity (there is more latitude in the construction of a sentence than in the composition of a word). Only the assumption of an intermediate level of abstraction in the interior of *langue* – a level of potentiality of the sequences that will be realized in *parole* – reconciles both these aspects. This supposes a distinction within the sentence between what pertains to *langue* ('the general type we have in mind', EC, 2079B) and what pertains to *parole* (the execution).

Saussure does not stop at this first type of relations. Associations are produced outside the chain of discourse in which a word recalls other words with which it has relations of various kinds ('this word will summon up in an unconscious fashion . . . the idea of a crowd of other words which, *in one way or another*, have something in common with it. Maybe in very different ways', EC, 2026E). Thus the word *enseignement* ('teaching') will evoke *enseigner* ('teach'), *renseigner* ('acquaint'), *apprentissage* ('apprenticeship'), *armement* ('armament'), etc. etc. All these relations – unordered and said to exist *in absentia* in so far as they are never co-present in a chain – are termed *associative relations* by Saussure.

Associative relations are presented as facts of memory: 'Their seat is in the brain', they constitute 'a potential mnemonic series', and form part of the 'inner storehouse' (p. 123) – so many ways of expressing their abstract character ('psychological' or 'potential', in Saussure's terms).

As well as possessing the faculty of making these associations, speaking subjects are capable of grasping their mechanism: they 'analyse' (with what degree of consciousness?) the character of the relation thus instituted. Here, for example, represented in the form of a network around *enseignement* ('teaching') are the terms which can be associated with it (p. 126):

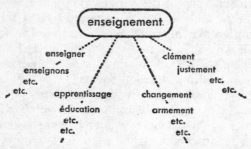

Speaking subjects clearly do not confuse the kind of relation instituted by each of the branches: (1) a relation established at the level of the radical; (2) a relation between the signifieds of the whole of the word; (3) mode of construction and similar suffixes (starting from a verbal root); (4) relationship at the level of the pure signifier (rhyme), abstracting from the grammatical relation. Moreover, nothing requires the associative series to stop there: 'The number of associative groups is infinite' (EC, 2033C).

The fourth series of the diagram merits a comment. As is well known, it was added by the editors. However, this was not an illegitimate move, for in his course Saussure had offered a similar example – the German *durchbläuen* (consigned to a note in the CGL, pp. 126–7). Contrary to etymology, *durchbläuen* ('to thrash') is associated with *blau*, because of the bruises caused by the blows. In Chapter 7 we shall return to the significance of the existence of such associations at the level of the pure signifier and the importance of linguistic theory encompassing them. A series of this kind is irreducible to grammar. Thus when Saussure later studies the link between the system of associations and that of grammar, founded on the subjects' awareness of it, and states that 'the sum of the conscious and methodical classifications made by the grammarian ... must coincide with the associations, conscious or not, that are set up in speaking' (pp. 137–38), his reasoning is based exclusively on the relations between *enseignement* and *enseigner* ('teach') on the one hand, *enseignement* and *jugement* ('judgment') on the other. Series 2 and series 4 are no longer in question: being beyond linguistic description, the association of signifieds and the association of signifiers have alike disappeared.

Thus a term finds itself at the centre of a constellation – a point of convergence for terms which 'float' around it. Hence *langue* can be seen as a kind of 'net hung over the whole of the material for signifying' (note 15.9, CFS 17).

The idea of association was to be taken up by Saussure's structuralist successors in the form of 'paradigm'. But the paradigm is more limited than association (cf., for example, the distributionalists' 'paradigmatic class'). Since the elements in paradigmatic relation have equivalent grammatical roles, association in the broad sense, and the multiplicity of relations which it offers, are lost.

The two axes can certainly be contrasted term by term, but the essential thing is that they not be considered in isolation: they condition each other reciprocally, and the sequence results from their interaction.

The dual existence of linguistic units (according to the associative and syntagmatic spheres) makes it possible to return to what was regarded as an aporia in the definition of the concrete unit: the fact that an element could appear in a double guise and yet constitute a single element (e.g., *dans*, with its two forms of $[\partial\tilde{a}]$ and $[\partial\tilde{a}z]$. Depending on whether one adopts a syntagmatic or an associative perspective the elements will be perceived differently.

3. The linguistic mechanism

It remains to show how the two spheres come into play complementarily in the production of the spoken chain. This is done by comparing chains which both contain constant elements of meaning and form and elements varying in meaning and form. This mechanism of intuitive comparison of series of sequences substantiates speakers' evident awareness of the unit: 'The syntagm can only be produced if we are aware of all the differences or oppositions the group of associations may present' (EC, 2063E).

Take the syntagm *dé-faire* ('un-do'), which is based upon two associative series. The first serves to isolate the prefix *dé-*; it consists of the forms *dé-coller* ('unstick'), *dé-placer* ('move'), etc. – but not *désirer* ('desire'), which would leave a non-existent radical. The second serves to isolate the radical *-faire*, starting from *faire* ('do'), *re-faire* ('redo'), *par-faire* ('perfect'), and *contre-faire* ('counterfeit'). Thus we see that it is the possibility of association which creates the syntagmatic bond: a syntagm only exists because there is an association ('To the extent that the other terms float around *défaire* . . ., [it] can be decomposed into subunits', p. 129). Consequently, should the series *décoller* or the series *refaire* disappear from the language, *défaire* would no longer be analysable into *dé-faire*.

Thus Saussure offers some thoughts on the way in which meaning is constituted in *langue*. A form is not selected because it signifies what one has to say, but according to a more complex process, whose foundation is differential: 'In reality the idea evokes not a form but a whole *latent system* that makes possible the *oppositions necessary* for the formation of the sign' (p. 130; my emphasis). The sign, or the sytagm into whose composition it enters, stands at the intersection of several associative series. In the application of this principle, there is no discontinuity between words (whether simple or not) – traditionally the domain of lexicology or morphology – and the sentence – the domain of syntax: 'This principle applies to even the most complex types of syntagms and sentences' (p. 130).

The entire linguistic system may be understood in terms of this interplay of syntagmatic and associative relations, which constitutes a veritable grammar. This has two consequences for grammatical method:

– One observes that speaking subjects possess a grammatical knowledge. Hence one can connect the 'subjective analysis' which they spontaneously practise when using their language (strictly synchronic) and the 'objective analysis' of the grammarian, who in addition possesses knowledge of the history of the language. The two analyses generally converge, for the objective analysis is simply the subjective made explicit. But they can diverge: in *enfant* ('child'), it is no longer possible synchronically to perceive the Latin elements *in-fans* ('one who does not speak'), nor, in *enceinte* ('pregnant'), *in-cincta* ('without a girdle'). Only the subjective analysis is 'based directly on the facts of language [*langue*]' (p. 183), and that is why it is accorded primacy in synchronic study.

– All synchronic facts are fundamentally of the same kind, and no obvious distinction is called for between lexicology and grammar: 'Only the distinction ... between syntagmatic and associative relations can provide a classification that is not imposed from the outside. No other base will serve for the grammatical system' (p. 136).

Thus conceived as a simultaneous activation of two types of relation, the linguistic mechanism makes it possible to return to the question of the unit, and especially the problem of defining it, assuming that we are not content simply to divide it into a succession of concrete words. Only an analysis capable of grasping the system as a whole allows us to see beneath a word such as *mois* ('month') a combination of the lexical unit *mois* and a marker (singular or plural). Moreover, to say that *cheval* and *chevaux* ('horses(s)') are the same word presupposes the following analysis: *cheval* = CHEVAL + the singular; *chevaux* = CHEVAL + the plural. Thus it involves an abstraction: 'We ask what *cheval* and *chevaux* have in common and we make an abstraction. Hence it is no longer a concrete unit' (EC, 1730 D).

This abstraction is required because the resultant of *all* the possible associations does not figure in linear fashion in the chain: 'The meaning of the word is fixed because it is surrounded by analogues which make the partial meaning visible by furnishing a series of new units inferior to the word' (EC, 2081 B).

4. The living units beneath words

One difficulty involved in the division into concrete units is those cases where simple segmentation is insufficient to guarantee the identification of values (e.g., the French pair *plaire/plu* 'rain'/'rained' or the English *take/took*).

In *plaire/plu* (an example from the sources which does not feature in the CGL), there is no materially segmentable signifier to ensure the association between the two forms (as there is, for example, in *chanter/chanté* 'sing'/'sung'). It can only be analysed by reference to the rest of the system. To the 'syntagmatic solidarity' legible in a material segment Saussure opposes 'associative solidarity' (EC, 2105 B): *plaire* and *plu* are related by 'associative delimitation'. Because of the parallelism of the oppositions the mechanism can be activated (*plaire/plu* is parallel to *chanter/chanté*).

Saussure uses the example of the Latin genitive to show that a segmental identity is not required to found the identity of value. Nothing in the form of the genitives *domin-i* ('of the master'), *reg-is* ('of the King'), and *ros-arum* ('of the roses') necessitates (or even permits) their assimilation. But these forms 'are connected by the feeling that they have a common value which prescribes an identical function. *This suffices to create the association* in the absence of any material support' (p. 138; my emphasis). It is thus that grammatical notions are elaborated – beyond material similarity, by the association of series in the speaker's awareness.

This analysis has two implications:

– In the case of what grammar traditionally calls suppletion, a single value may have different material supports (cf. *aller* 'go' in French, which speakers encounter in *vont* 'they go', *ira* 'he will go', *allons* 'we go', etc. etc.).

– A single segment, unamenable to linear decomposition, may be the expression of more than one value. For example, in the case of the English *men* it would be absurd to say that it is the *e* which expresses the plural: a comparison with other English plurals indicates that *men*, which cannot be broken down, is to be understood as *man* + the plural.

Facts pertaining to alternation all suppose interpretation by association. Alternation is a phonetic phenomenon in which a regular modification acquires a grammatical significance (as in the German series *geben/gibt* 'give', *helfen/hilft* 'help', *nehmen/nimmt* 'take' . . . or *beissen/biss* 'bite', *reiten/ritt* 'ride'. . .). Vocalic alternation 'does not impair the unity of language [*langue*] because it is regulated' (EC, 2408D). Reducing these forms to a unit by means of a rule, speakers do not perceive them as irregular, because the opposition appears significant to them.

Once it is acknowledged that not all the oppositions to which a word gives rise necessarily appear in the sequence, it may be analysed as the junction of several series. Thus in the Latin verb form *legimus* (an example from the sources) are to be found: the radical *legere* (because the form is not *habemus*); present (/*legebamus*); indicative (/*legamus*); active (/*legemur*); first person (/*legitis*); plural (/*lego*). It is impossible to attribute a material segment to each of these units. Nevertheless, they genuinely exist, albeit non-materially, for without them the analysis of *legimus* would alter. But their mode of existence is not material, but potential.

But do the units thus extracted really exist in the awareness of speaking subjects – and not just for the grammarian? Through the system they acquire sufficient reality for Saussure to refer to 'units living underneath the word' (EC, 2780 B): 'living', in so far as they are felt to be significant by speakers.

The grammatical category of a word is likewise established by the associative series: 'Cf. associative series in the fact that, as a substantive, *enseignement* is related to other substantives' (EC, 2028 E). Thus association affords access to the grammatical.

5. Relative motivation

In Chapter 3 we saw that Saussure conceived relative arbitrariness as a 'restriction' or 'reduction' of radical arbitrariness by the system.

He demonstrates the role of relative motivation by a *reductio ad absurdum*, proposing the hypothetical example of a language which only possesses simple signs (or a purely semiological organization, without syntax): 'The different terms of this language would have no relations with each other, would remain as separate as the objects themselves' (EC, 2105 F). An imaginary language of this kind would be related to actual languages: its terms would definitely have value, since they would still be relative to one another. But the fact that no language is organized in this way underlines the role of relations and the relatively motivated, demonstrating that *langue* must not be treated as an exclusively semiological system. This point obviously bears on words, for sentences are by definition analysable, composed of the relatively motivated. Words and sentences put the relatively motivated in play, and thus morphology and syntax are not fundamentally different in kind.

This hypothetical example having been dealt with, when *langue* is taken as it is, signs exhibit an organization accounted for by relative arbitrariness, which links the signifying character to availability for the analogical process. Thus it may be noted that the prefix *sé-* of *séduire* ('seduce'), *séparer* ('separate'), or *sélection* ('selection') is not analogically productive; it is not significant for speakers (see 6.7 below).

So signs can be divided into two groups: a complex sign (analysable) is relatively motivated (e.g., *poir-ier* or *dix-neuf*) and a simple sign (unanalysable) is absolutely arbitrary (e.g., *poire* or *dix*). But (as intuition immediately suggests) this would appear implicitly to concede that the only analysis possible is syntagmatic in character. Taking into account what we have just seen, if we do not wish to treat *plu* differently from *chanté* it will be necessary to extend relative motivation to signs which are analysable because of signifying parallelism.

The sources are a valuable aid in reading the highly elliptical section on 'Absolute and Relative Arbitrariness' (pp. 131ff.). In Engler three of the four columns of student notes contain the same comment: 'The solidarity of the terms in the system may be conceived as a restriction of arbitrariness, be it syntagmatic solidarity or associative solidarity' (EC, 2106 B, with *plaire/plu* as an example of associative limitation). This statement (and especially the example) is clearer than the CGL, where we simply find: 'now we recognize the solidarities that bind them [the units]; they are associative and syntagmatic, and they are what limits arbitrariness' (p. 133).

Nevertheless, the CGL (and Course III, from which this passage derives) attends at greater length to syntagmatic motivation. In part this is doubtless for pedagogical reasons: syntagmatic motivation is more obvious, because it is visible segmentally (it only involves segmental concrete units). But it is clear that the whole of the preceding analysis militates against restricting oneself exclusively to the segmental.

Even so, broadening the analysis could lead to an impasse: since *all* signs are at the centre of an associative constellation, since *all* terms are an intersection of relations, should not even unanalysable signs be considered relatively motivated? Not if we wish to preserve the idea of grammar, and a linguist cannot be induced to treat *poire* on the one hand, *poirier* or *men* on the other, in identical manner. The distinction between motivated signs and unmotivated signs facilitates a new approach to the question of the respective domains of lexicology and grammar. Saussure demonstrates the limitations of a simple equation: *lexicology = unmotivated* and *grammar = relatively motivated* (see Chapter 7), but stresses that it is theoretically fertile:

– Creativity does not follow the same pattern in the order of the unmotivated and that of the relatively motivated. Lexical values pertain to non-closed series, to which an element can always be added. Grammatical values pertain to finite series (new suffixes or tenses are rarely created in a language), on the basis of which an infinite number of signs may be formed. In French, for example, the addition of suffix *-eur* to a verbal root can serve for the creation of numerous nouns and, in particular, of a new noun on the basis of a new verb. 'The lexicological instrument being composed of isolated compartments, the grammatical instrument being like a chain formed of links bound to one another, wherein one unit demands the other' (EC, 2119 E).

– A typology of languages can be envisaged, according to the part allotted each of these two orders. Each language may be classified between 'a minimum of organization and a minimum of arbitrariness' (p. 133), the extremes being inconceivable. Returning to the same problem later, Saussure also refers to the proportion of 'productive and sterile words' (p. 166). In order to illustrate a typology based upon the role of the relatively motivated, he proposes a descending order of Sanskrit (where the role of the motivated is not important), then Latin, German, French, English and Chinese.

6. Abstract entities

Given Saussure's reticence about abstraction at the end of a positivist century, it is worth emphasizing that he devotes a whole chapter to 'abstract' units, which he contrasts with concrete units as follows: 'We have reserved the term *concrete* for cases where the idea has a direct basis in a sound-unit, whereas the *abstract* has an indirect basis as a result of an *operation* on the part of speakers' (EC, 2195E).

Abstract entities refer to everything on the part of speakers which displays a capacity to analyse the associations they are liable to produce. In associating *enseignement* on the one hand to *enseigner* and, on the other, to *jugement*, they possess the faculty of attributing a different signification to each of these associations: 'we glimpse a link between association and grammar' (EC, 2172 B).

Starting from the absence of material similarity between the three marks of the Latin genitive *domin-i*, *reg-is* and *ros-arum* (see p. 99), Saussure demonstrates that a grammatical category can be constituted without any material support, via 'the feeling that they have a common value which prescribes an identical functioning' (p. 138).

Whether genitive, substantive, or any other grammatical category, abstract entities are obtained by transition from particular concrete elements to the general class which they constitute. This involves an operation of abstraction. If (despite Saussure's own reservations) one considers the transition from *parole* to *langue* as abstraction, leading the linguist from realized elements to their underlying schema, it might even be said that this is a second level of abstraction. A second abstraction wherein the material support is abandoned and the speakers' consciousness of a common value highlighted – an awareness which creates an existence as powerful as that possessed by the material segments. '*Langue* knows nothing of the terms 'radical', 'suffix', etc. But its awareness and utilization of these differences cannot be denied' (EC, 2180 B).

The role of awareness is very important in Saussure, and we have already encountered it in the definition of synchrony (p. 51). Subsequent twentieth-century linguists will likewise appeal to it when they refer to the 'awareness of the speaking subject' or the 'intuition of the native speaker'. The only restriction that might be placed upon its utilization concerns the relation between it and the grammarian's analysis: it may be asked whether 'the awareness of speakers goes as far as the analyses of the grammarian' (p. 138) and how explicit it can be for the subjects themselves.

Nevertheless, the purchase of this principle is limited by the relationship between the abstract entities and material realizations: '*abstract entities are always based, in the last analysis, on concrete entities*' (p. 138). This sentence is rather obscure, but the sources are more explicit: 'We see that in the final analysis we shall always have to return to identities or entities of the kind we have defined. Study of the concrete entities will always have to come first, and everything will rest upon these units' (EC, 2184 B). This indicates both that study of the abstract entities is an ultimate operation of grammar and that it directly or indirectly supposes the possibility of the linguist basing him- or herself upon some concrete segment.

The phenomenon of word-order is likewise an abstract unit, in so far as '*langue* abstracts it by analysis, as well as the units themselves' (EC, 2189B). This applies equally to the order of elements in the word (*désir-eux*, 'desirous', not *eux-desir*) and the order of words in the sentence, about which there are two things to be stressed. First, a relation can be expressed by simple juxtaposition – something demonstrated by comparing languages (cf. the English *gold watch* and the French *montre en or*) or different states of the same language (it is *Hôtel-Dieu* in Old French, whilst modern French insists on the preposition *de*). Secondly, inversion of the order can change the meaning (compare *je dois* 'I must' and *dois-je* 'must I?'). Word-order (a feature common to all languages – even those said to have a free word-order) is directly connected to the linearity of the signifier. As in the case of abstract entities of the first type, the fact that they have a basis in concrete units is decisive here, and reveals one of the properties of syntax. 'To think that there is an incorporeal syntax outside material units distributed in space would be a mistake' (p. 139). This is proved by the English example *the man I have seen*, wherein French speakers tend to see a zero-sign because of the absence of what French translates by *que* (*l'homme que j'ai vu*). But it is the translation which engenders the illusion 'that nothingness can express something', for it is the form of the grouping that produces its value.

The notion of abstract entity is very important in Saussure: a unit of *langue* inaccessible without analysis, it nevertheless possesses the same reality in the understanding of the linguistic mechanism as the concrete unit, because of the role it performs for speakers. Saussure's postulation of it serves both to corroborate his analysis of the concrete unit and to ward against the two dangers which seemed to him to pose the greatest threat to any understanding of the linguistic: granting an existence to the material unit solely on the basis of its materiality, without referring to value, on the one hand; and assuming that abstractions are non-material, forgetting that a meaning only exists with the support of a material form, on the other.

7. Analogy, functioning, creativity

In view of the distinction between synchrony and diachrony, at first sight it may appear incongruous to connect the language mechanism and analogy. And the latter, which concerns change, is defined in the third part of the CGL ('Diachronic Linguistics').

In fact, the association is only surprising if analogy is understood in the traditional sense. This is what Saussure himself does in Course I. But from Course II onwards he so broadens it that its role in a synchronic perspective becomes visible. Unfortunately, since the CGL is here a composite of these two courses (analogy not being discussed in Course III), it is not always easy to bring out the innovations contained in the second.

Analogy is initially defined as one of the manifestations of linguistic change, as opposed to phonetic change, from which it differs particularly in its effects.

Phonetic change is the natural and constant evolution which modifies the form of a word – for example, from the Latin *calidum* to the French *chaud* ('hot'), via the steps *calidu, caldu, cald, calt*, [tʃalt], [tʃaut), [ʃaut], [ʃot], [ʃo]. It has two effects; it loosens the grammatical links, and it strengthens them. The attenuation of the grammatical link has repercussions on value. First, a word is no longer felt synchronically to be derived from another (thus in French *berger* 'shepherd' no longer bears any relation to *brebis* 'ewe', unlike the Latin *berbicarius*, which is derived from *berbix*). Secondly – and correlatively – the parts of a word cease to analysable (cf. the French *enemi* with the Latin *in-imicus* 'enemy', where the link with *amicus* 'friend' is evident). Thus in the transition from the Latin to the French the degree of relative motivation decreases. By contrast, a strengthening of the grammatical links is apparent when a regular phonetic modification is invested in a grammatical regularity. This is alternation.

To the extent that it does not produce alternation, phonetic change is therefore a factor of grammatical disturbance: absolute arbitrariness prevails over relative arbitrariness, and 'the linguistic mechanism is obscured' (p. 161). However, these effects are counter-balanced by the action of analogy.

Saussure defines analogy in four stages: a definition, some examples, a diagram, and a comparison. The definition: 'Analogy supposes a model and its regular imitation. *An analogical form is a form made on the model of one or more other forms in accordance with a definite rule*' (p. 161). The sources specify that 'Another form created by association is substituted for an existing traditional form' (EC, 2460 B). Among several examples, let us take the Latin *honor*, whose appearance is explained with the help of the diagram of the so-called proportional fourth:

$$\text{oratorem: orator} = \text{honorem : x}$$
$$\text{x} = \text{honor}$$

This is to be read as follows : on the model of the pair *oratorem/orator*, Latin analogically creates the regularized form *honor*, whereas the hereditary nominative is *honos*.

The comparison is a drama with a cast of three: the legitimate form *honos*; the rival *honor*; and 'a collective character made up of the forms that created the rival (*honorem, orator, oratorem*, etc.)' (p. 163). The diagram demonstrates that the legitimate form has no hand in the action. Thus analogy is more than a change; it is an innovation wherein a distinction must be made between the stages of the creation of a new form and the disappearance of the old, which falls into disuse as a result of its irregularity. Furthermore, the innovations of analogy can replace nothing, as in the case of *répressionnaire* ('one who favours repression'), which might be created on the model of *reaction/réactionnaire* ('reaction'/'reactionary').

In offering an analysis already to be found in the neo-grammarians together with a notion borrowed from Greek grammar, Saussure adds nothing new. By contrast, the presentation of analogy as an entirely grammatical and synchronic phenomenon, assimilable to the ordinary mechanism of *langue*, is radically new. Like the language mechanism, analogy assumes 'awareness and understanding of a relation between forms' (p. 165). The play of *langue*, the latent analysis which it presupposes, makes both ordinary usage and analogical formations possible. The diagram of the fourth proportional serves to present analogy as well as significant parallelisms:

Plaire : plu = chanter : chanté.

An analogical creation like *indécorable* simply reassembles elements that exist elsewhere, but are not yet grouped into a syntagm. Its constellation might comprise: *décor-er* ('decorate'), *décor-ation*, ('decoration'); *pardonn-able* ('pardonable'), *maniable* ('manageable'); *in-connu* ('unknown'), *in-sensé* ('insane'). . . *Langue* itself contains the potential for its own creation, and 'realizing it in speaking [*parole*] is a small matter in comparison with the build-up of forces that makes it possible' (p. 166). For the study of the functioning of *langue*, analogy is therefore a complementary aspect of the interplay of relations in the mechanism.

Indirectly, analogy likewise confirms the distinction between *langue* and *parole*. If its activation presupposes an analysis of *langue*, its realization is 'the chance product of an isolated speaker' (p. 165), a fact of *parole*. The role of each order, although linked, is distinct: 'Creative activity will simply be a combinatory activity – the creation of new combinations. But a combination constructed out of what materials? They are not given from outside; *langue* must derive them from itself. This is why the first act of analysis was required: *langue* spends its time interpreting and decomposing the contribution of previous generations in order then to combine new constructions with the subunits thus obtained' (EC, 2573 B). The role of the individual in analogical creation is evident in the existence of ephemeral combinations, such as the mistakes made by children (e.g., *viendre* formed on the basis of *viendrai*, by analogy with *éteindre/éteindrai*).

The *langue/parole* distinction is thus confirmed at the price of being jumbled with another idea: just as *langue* changes by *parole*, so in analogy a role is accorded to the intervention of speakers in a process of *langue*. This might be considered a regression vis-à-vis the definition of the linguistic, corresponding to the fact that, elaborated in Course II, Saussure's thoughts on analogy represent a less finished problematic than that at work in the section on 'Synchronic Linguistics', which is drawn entirely from Course III.

The final characteristic of analogy is that it is a factor of conservation, as well as innovation, in *langue*. As we have seen, it is innovative since it is a process of creation, and potentially of infinite creation, whatever its relation to reality. Saussure takes the example of the German *Elephantlein* (a diminutive formed thanks to the suffix -*lein*, on the model of *Fraülein*) which is linguistically legitimate though scarcely plausible. But it is also a factor of conservation, for it makes something new with the available material, which it redistributes: 'Language [*langue*] is a garment covered with patches cut from its own cloth' (p. 172) Moreover, it confirms the ordinary functioning of the mechanism, for the stability of forms is bound up with

93

the fact that they are framed in the system and a form is transmitted intact in so far as it is analysable. Saussure uses the image of a 'procession of associated forms'* which retains its unity all along its route. In this respect, analogy coincides with the mechanism perfectly: 'Forms are . . . preserved because they are constantly renewed by analogy' (p. 172).

Analogy therefore plays a significant part in Saussure's theoretical constructions: the key point of the relations as the mobilization of the associative in the syntagmatic, it is also at the interface between two basic dichotomies – the bridge between synchrony and diachrony and between *langue* and *parole*. It is one of the ways in which Saussure accounts for creativity – a zone which he is only able to enter by assuming that the position of the subject blurs the distinction between *langue* and *parole* (see 5.5).

Saussure suggests that the grammarian credits *langue* with an organization as subtle as that revealed in its utilization by speakers: 'If the mass of forms which make up *langue* for each individual simply remained a chaos in their heads, *parole* and *langue* would alike be inconceivable. The necessity of a classification, of some order, is an *a priori* necessity even in the absence of psychology' (EC, 2024 B). With the model of relations, which endows the mechanism whereby each sign summons up a potentially infinite chain of associations with real depth, we are a long way from the initial presentation of the sign as a simple bond between signifier and signified. Therewith a model is installed in which grammar's ambitions are equal to the variegated play of *langue*, as revealed by the use its speakers make of it.

Thus Saussure seems to open up interesting lines of argument pertaining to what would now be called the relations between *langue* and unconscious. In the next chapter we shall examine what this entails in terms of grammar, for the two objectives are manifestly not one and the same.

* The French phrase 'cortège de formes associées' (*CLG*, p. 236) is omitted from the English translation [translator's note].

THE MECHANISM

Further Reading

CGL:
Part II, chapters V, VI, VII, VIII
Part III, chapters II, III, IV, V

René Amacker, *Linguistique saussurienne*, Droz, Geneva 1975.
Oswald Ducrot, 'Le Structuralisme en linguistique', *Qu'est-ce que le structuralisme?*, Seuil, Paris 1969.
Oswald Ducrot and Tzvetan Todorov, *Encyclopedic Dictionary of the Sciences of Language* (article on Syntagma and Paradigm), Basil Blackwell, Oxford 1979.
Claudine Haroche, Paul Henry and Michel Pêcheux, 'La Sémantique et la coupure saussurienne', *Langages* 24, 1971.

7

The Play of the Signifier

Value and relations in play in the mechanism are the point at which Saussure's work touches the limits of the grammatical: what is the relation between certain operations in the production of meaning and grammar? With these limits we encounter the contradictions in Saussure and it is especially important to distinguish between Course I and Course III.

In order to pinpoint this contradiction in the CGL, we are going to take a detour via Saussure's other works, for our aim is to show that the contradiction is not between the CGL and the 'other Saussure', but *inside* the CGL *and* the other works.

Let us begin with the *Anagrams*. Encapsulating the distinction between the *Anagrams* and the CGL in the metaphor of day and night implies that the latter have nothing in common with the CGL. And it is indeed the case that only a single concept figures in both problematics: linearity, which is proposed in the CGL and challenged by the *Anagrams* – as can be seen in the example of Scipio (see p. 15).

What do the *Anagrams* tell us about *langue*? We have seen (Chapter 1) that they concerned the exploration of a poetic procedure. Astonished by the 'stream' of anagrams in texts, Saussure initially did his utmost to see in them a conscious procedure, wondering whether they were '*deliberately and consciously applied*' or 'purely fortuitous' (WUW, p. 118). But this dichotomy was exploded when he realized that he was discovering anagrams everywhere: 'I have tried in vain, by opening the book randomly at all possible places . . ., to find a passage without these figures' (p. 86). Saussure was forced to recognize the general character of the phenomenon and the impossibility of escaping it: 'If it exists, [this law] becomes the inevitable basis – by nature deplorable, but inescapable – which will determine for almost any passage the form of words which the author gives his thoughts' (p. 102). He cannot resist treating this abundance as pathological: 'this affection which assumed pathological proportions once the thing was extended to the simple expression of thoughts in a letter . . . volumes . . . were literally bathed in inescapable hypograms' (p. 86).[1] Their abundance in poetry and some prose works was one thing. But in Caesar's commentaries or Cicero's informal letters! Saussure set about a frantic search for 'proof', even writing to a contemporary poet whose Saturnian poetry was replete with anagrams. When no reply was forthcoming, he simply abandoned his research.

Saussure's reasoning might be reconstructed as follows: if, as their abundance would tend to suggest, anagrams are not intentional, then, outside of *langue* as pure form, the signifier must be credited with a materiality, substance with a weight. This is to glimpse an infinity to *langue* – that everything in it is not homogeneous, that the sign is not transparent, that the subject is not master of *langue*. . . His confusion leads him to write: 'One cannot speak of anagrams as of a game which is accessory to the versification. They become the foundation of that versification, whether the poet wishes it or not, whether the critic on the one hand, and the versifier on the other wish it or not' (p. 17.) Giving up the research seems to have been the only way in which Saussure could react to an inextricable conflict, at a time when he was beginning to teach general linguistics.

Some ten years previously, Saussure had already confronted the relations between *langue* and unconscious, in his encounter with the glossolalia of the clairvoyant Mlle Smith. How could one explain the ability of a Swiss villager – who only knew French, a little German and a smattering of Hungarian from her father – to express herself in a language which wasn't Sanskrit, but which 'never [has] an anti-Sanskrit character, i.e. [does] not present groups materially contrary or opposed to the general figure of the Sanskrit words' (IPM, p. 269)? As with the *Anagrams* ten years later, Saussure oscillates between two extremes. Either he robs the phenomenon of any originality by making it a fortuitous effect ('the rule her mind obeys is that these familiar words must each be replaced by an exotic-sounding substitute. It scarcely matters how' – p. 270). Or, when meticulously examining her productions, he implicitly accepts the inexplicable – thereby conceding that it may have been Sanskrit.

Saussure's ambivalence towards the phenomenon is highlighted by the fact that he was sufficiently fascinated to help Flournoy (who did not know Sanskrit) by composing a text 'Latin in appearance, that would be to the language of Livy or Cicero as nearly as possible what the Sanskrit of Simandini[2] is to that of the Brahmans'. Here we find our austere scholar busily coining dog Latin!

A contemporary linguist demonstrated that it was possible to escape the dilemma of coincidence or inexplicability. Saussure had noted that Mlle Smith's 'Hindu' productions were marked by the absence of the consonant *ʃ*, which does not actually exist in Sanskrit, but which, had she proceeded at random, she could not have failed to produce. But his only explanation was a mediumistic knowledge of Sanskrit. Returning to the problem subsequently, the French linguist Victor Henry[3] advanced a suggestion which requires *langue* being credited with another dimension than that of the code: the absence of the *ʃ* derived from the care Mlle Smith took not to model her productions on French.[4] Regardless of whether this explanation is correct, it assumes that by association one term can refer to some other. This is precisely what Saussure was not yet ready to propose; the idea would only be advanced in Course III.

In this first encounter with the symbolic, as in the second, Saussure comes close to recognizing that not everything concerning *langue* is explained by *langue* – and turns away from what he has glimpsed.

From 1907 Saussure began to teach general linguistics. What is the relationship between this teaching and his other intellectual concerns? We can assume that the contradictions which have just been highlighted will reappear here.

In Chapters 3, 4, 5 and 6 the fundamental points of Saussurian theory have been examined. For present purposes they can be resumed in a few propositions:

- Every act of *parole* brings into play a latent system whose functioning escapes immediate observation – as a result of its abstract organization, of the fact that speakers are not aware of its mechanisms, and of the fragmentary nature of its realizations compared with its potential. The system's mode of existence is such that it is impossible to theorize *langue* without assuming its existence, without assuming that its substance remains inert until such time as a system endows it with form.

- A network of notions is elaborated around the system: synchrony, difference, opposition, value – abstract notions which challenge the idea of thought pre-existing *langue*, of origin and of a hierarchy of values.

- The system creates values by the interplay of two axes of relations at work in every act of *parole*: the syntagmatic relation and the associative relation, which reflect the 'analysis' conducted by speakers when they speak. The workings of association, and its theoretically infinite character, make it poss-ible to understand what is said as having its basis in the latent and unspoken.

- These propositions are essential to the elaboration of hypotheses on the way in which creative *parole* is constructed, on how meaning occurs in what is said. . . However, although they designate the limitations of grammar by exploring the functioning of the relations governed by the code, they do not go beyond it, since they can still be described in its terms.

But although rare, there are points in the CGL which concern phenomena that elude grammar and demonstrate that another motivation – one beyond grammatical (relative) motiv-ation – can be envisaged, which I shall call symbolic.

One of these concerns the 'fourth branch' of the diagram of associations (see 6.2), the association of the pure signifier – *clément* and *justement*, associated with *enseignement*. In Course I Saussure had accepted only those associations which involve both sides of the sign simultaneously; he condemned any other association as 'unilateral'. But in Course III the perspective is broadened, and the simile for association changes from a star to a constellation: 'A word can always evoke *everything* that can be associated with it *in one way or another* (p. 126; my emphasis). And every term refers '*in one respect or another*' (EC, 2026 E) to the other terms of the language. A constellation is 'the point of convergence of an indefinite number of co-ordinated terms' (p. 126), and this coordination can occur via the ensemble of the sign or by the signified or signifier alone. Whether *durchbläuen* or *clément* and *justement*, associations at the level of the pure signifier have the particularity of eluding meaning. They also meet with some reluctance on the part of the editors[5]: in the note to which *durchbläuen* is relegated, they write that 'the last case is rare and can be classed as abnormal, for the mind naturally discards associations that becloud the intelligibility of discourse'. And they add: 'But its existence is proved by a lower category of puns based on the ridiculous confusions that can result from pure and simple homonomy. . .' (pp. 126–27 n.).

Nothing in the notes betrays a value judgement on Saussure's part and one has the impression that the CGL exhibits several contradictions here – Course I versus Course III, Saussure versus himself, the editors versus Saussure – the whole leading to a limitation of the idea that the mechanism functions beyond grammar. Disapproval of this fourth branch is not restricted to the editors; it can also be found in Godel, a linguist of great subtlety, when he criticizes them for having 'added to the diagram of associative relations the spurious series *enseignement*, *clément*, *justement*, etc., which has no right to be there' (SM, p. 248). The stakes are unquestionably high: if there is a symbolic motivation which exceeds grammatical motivation, *langue* in its entirety is not the preserve of the linguist.

There is another phenomenon irreducible to grammar, which appears to induce the same hesitancy on Saussure's part and the same reticence on the editors': folk etymology. Folk etymology designates an innovation in *langue* resulting from 'attempts to explain refractory words by relating them to something known' (p. 173): 'In this way Old French *coute-pointe* (from *coute*, variant of *couette*, "cover", and *pointe*, past participle of *poindre*, "quilt") was changed to *courtepointe* "counterpane", as if formed from the adjective *court* "short" and the noun *pointe* "point" ' (p. 173). The character of innovation by folk etymology is clarified by a comparison with analogy. Common to both is their employment of significant elements furnished by the language. But whereas analogy involves the disappearance of the earlier form, folk etymology is a reinterpretation of the old form. Analogy can therefore affect all words, whilst folk etymology only affects a few technical or foreign words recalcitrant to spontaneous analysis, and involves 'interpretations of misunderstood forms in terms of known forms' (p. 175).

The CGL is very disparaging about folk etymology. Whilst analogy and folk etymology can produce similar innovations (e.g., *sourdité* 'deafness' could be formed by analogy as well as by interpretation), there is a disparity in the presentation: analogy is said to proceed in a rational fashion; folk etymology, by contrast, works 'somewhat haphazardly and results only in absurdities' (p. 174). In fact, the real difference lies elsewhere. In copying, analogy does not deviate from the full diagram of the sign, wherein the signifier has a signified as its counterpart. In assigning a role to the substance of the signifier, folk etymology, on the other hand, eludes grammar. Thus like associations of signifiers, folk or latent etymology demonstrates that two terms with a different signification may have something in common at the level of value – something irreducible to grammatical association. This means that *langue* has to be recognized as having a latent mechanism that functions beneath what is said, that it operates outside the grammatical mechanism, and that motivation by the system extends to the point that everything can evoke everything, through any relation whatsoever.

Folk etymology and association of the signifier are tackled with the same hesitation as to whether they are normal or pathological. In Course I (the only source) Saussure's judgement on folk etymology conforms to that reproduced by the editors: 'There is something in it which may be regarded as perverted, pathological, albeit that it is a very particular instance of analogy' (EC, 2670 B). This encapsulates Saussure's hesitation: he is reluctant to consider the operation normal, and yet we perceive the emergence of what would have dictated the revision of the initial viewpoint in Course III (except that folk etymology is not discussed in it).

In this perspective, the rest of *langue*'s functioning is, by contrast, presented as normal. It is therefore the definition of notions that isolates the normal functioning of *langue*, and this has the effect of closing grammar in on itself and excluding ambiguity.

– Because it approaches *langue* in terms of what it has in common with other codes, the semiological viewpoint tends to treat it as a means for the expression of an idea, in direct contravention of the insistence on the absence of any ideas anterior to *langue*.

– When *langue* and *parole* are opposed as code and realization of the code, *parole*, which enables the speaker 'to express his personal thoughts', would appear to restore the precedence of the 'wishing-to-say' or 'meaning' (to say) [*vouloir-dire*] over the 'saying' [*dire*] – a perspective challenged in the definition of *langue* as value. *Parole* would reestablish the subject's mastery over his/her language.

– The mode of determination of the unit leads Saussure to abandon anything that cannot become a principle of classification, everything from which the unit cannot be extracted. Here Saussure is a veritable comparatist: whatever cannot be classified by relation to the identical is excluded from the field of linguistics.

– When form is opposed to substance, the weight of form conceals the substantial depth of the signifier, which is in danger of becoming pure transparency.

By concealing the evolution between the courses, the organization of the CGL makes it impossible to follow the evolution of the contradictions.

Saussure modified his position most radically between Course I and Course III on the subject of the relations, and especially association. In Course I association is limited by a restriction: 'At no stage does the consciousness of the speaking subjects relate two elements of identical sound with a different value' (SM, p. 59). The example given to illustrate the point is the impossibility of connecting *in-* in *inspirer* ('inspire') and in *inconnu* ('unknown'). Clearly, no grammatical reflection can be founded on such an association. Yet bearing as it does upon prefixes, this is precisely the case of the fourth branch (*enseignement/clément*)! Accordingly, this is in contradiction with Course III – as is the following characterization of the bond between signified and signifier, which appears in the CGL and derives from Course I: 'it is clear that only the associations sanctioned by that language appear to us to conform to reality, and we disregard whatever others might be imagined' (pp. 66–7). How is this locking mechanism on the side of the code ensured? Initially, Saussure only recognized associations which could be related to the awareness of speaking subjects.

It will be recalled that the 'recourse to awareness' was necessitated by the difficulties of linear delimitation. But we are in utter contradiction once more here: the same linguist who declared that 'the linguistic act is the least considered, the least premeditated, the most impersonal of all' (SM, p. 38), at the same time makes signifying capacity dependent upon degree of awareness.

Course III again supplies a decisive alteration: 'signifying capacity' (Course I) is therein replaced by 'degree of motivation', which accompanies the postulation of value and the displacement of the problematic from the sign to the system. Thus the possibility of an opening to the unconscious revolves around the relatively motivated, and especially the sphere of operations attributed to it.

The role of relative motivation is indeed cardinal. Linked to the syntagmatic when linear delimitation is possible (*poire – poirier*), relayed by the associative when it is not (*plaire – plu*), it raises the following question: given that every sign is in an associative relation with an infinite number of other signs that make up a constellation, are there such things as unmotivated signs? If the grammatical answer is yes (see 6.5), the symbolic answer is probably no, and it is imperative to distinguish carefully between grammatical motivation and symbolic motivation.

Thus there is in *langue* a point at which the knowledge offered by grammar ceases, where the possible associations no longer pertain to its order. This might be represented by a progression: *enseignement/armement* (grammatical paradigm); *enseignement/ justement* (different words containing two suffixes of similar form, but formed on the basis of different roots); *enseignement/ clément* (suffix in only one case, but similar graphic and phonic form); *enseignement/maman* (common feature only in the oral signifier). Grammar only comes into its own in the first case, having an ever decreasing role to play in the remainder. Saussurian linguistics is thus able to reveal something of how people speak, how creative *parole* is produced, thanks to a few crucial traits:

– *Langue* is cleansed of its imaginary attachments because it is without origin and because it is only relation and difference. The sign has no substance, no qualities of its own: difference is not a secondary quality of the sign; it is part of its very definition.

– The signifier only signifies its own power to signify. There is such a thing as 'plain meaning', as is evident from this example of Saussure's, quoted by Engler: 'Out walking, I make a notch in a tree without saying anything, just for the pleasure of it. The person with me remembers this notch, and she henceforth understandably associates two or three ideas with it, whereas I myself had no other idea in mind than to mystify her or amuse myself' (CFS, 19). It is the relations, syntagmatic and associative, which occasion a signification under a signifier.

– Nothing ensures that two speakers attribute the same meaning to the same segment. But this is not a problem, unless one believes in communication and a stable meaning – precisely what Saussure is wary of. He seeks to understand how *meaning*, whatever it may be, is produced.

In proposing that the linguist is not concerned with *langue* in its entirety, Saussure defines the linguist's position. He unquestionably traces the object of linguistics by 'discarding'; it is for others to do something with what is discarded – not the linguist, who need not as such know anything of it.

It would have been pleasing to conclude by listing the undisputed points of Saussurian linguistics, which would in some sense constitute the common property of linguists. But that is not possible. Literally all Saussure's concepts have aroused lively controversy. So, given that structuralist methodology is likewise subject to discussion, what remains of Saussure today?

There remains a reflection on the position of the linguist. From a whole variety of angles (psychoanalytical, pragmatic, cognitive, logical, etc. etc.), various disciplines (only partially similar to the 'related sciences' from which Saussure demar-

104

cated the linguistic viewpoint) currently aim to deal with language. Linguists can adopt one of two attitudes to this: those not reconciled to the idea that something pertaining to language [*langage ou de la langue*] should elude them, can compete with these disciplines on their own ground; alternatively, they can try to understand what constitutes the specificity of their practice (let the linguist know 'what he is doing').

In this respect Saussure's thought is more contemporary than ever.

Further Reading

CGL:
Part II, chapters V and VI
Part III, chapters VI and VII

Michel Arrivé, 'Intertexte et intertextualité chez F. de Saussure?', *Le Plaisir de l'intertexte: formes et fonctions de l'intertextualité dans le littérature française du XXe siècle*, Peter Lang, Paris 1986.
Claudine Normand, *Métaphore et concept*, Editions Complexe, Brussels 1976.
Moustapha Safouan, *L'Inconscient et son scribe*, Seuil, Paris 1982.
Beatrice Turpin, *Le Jeu de la langue chez Saussure*, thèse de 3e cycle Université de Paris X, 1980.
Tzvetan Todorov, *Theories of the Symbol*, Basil Blackwell, Oxford 1982.

Bibliography to Part One

The CGL and its sources:
Saussure, Ferdinand de, *Cours de linguistique générale*, critical edition prepared by T. de Mauro, Payot, Paris 1972.
——, *Course in General Linguistics*, trans. by Wade Baskin, Fontana, London 1974.
——, Notes inédites, *Cahiers Ferdinand de Saussure* (Geneva) 12, 1954.
——, 'Introduction au deuxième cours', *Cahiers Ferdinand de Saussure* 15, 1957.
Engler, Rudolf, *Edition critique du Cours de linguistique générale de Ferdinand de Saussure*, Otto Harrassowitz, Wiesbaden 1967–74.
Godel, Robert, *Les Sources manuscrites du Cours de linguistique générale*, Droz, Geneva 1957.

Other works by Saussure and commentaries:
Arrivé, Michel, *Linguistique et psychanalyse*, Klincksieck, Paris 1986.
——, 'Intertexte et intertextualité chez F. de Saussure?', *Le plaisir de l'intertexte: formes et fonctions de l'intertextualité dans la littérature française du XXe siècle*, Peter Lang, Paris 1986.
Flournoy, Théodore, *Des Indes à la planète Mars*, Seuil, Paris 1983.
Normand, Claudine, *Métaphore et concept*, Editions Complexe, Brussels 1976.
Rey, Jean-Michel, 'Saussure avec Freud', *Critique* 309, 1973.
Saussure, Ferdinand de, *Receuil des publications scientifiques*, Slatkine, Geneva-Paris 1984.
—— *Semiotexte*, I, 2 and II, 1, 1974–75, 'The Two Saussures'.
Safouan, Moustapha, *L'Inconscient et son scribe*, Seuil, Paris 1982.
Starobinski, Jean, *Words upon Words: The Anagrams of Ferdinand de Saussure*, Yale University Press, New Haven 1979.
Todorov, Tzvetan, *Theories of the Symbol*, Basil Blackwell, Oxford, 1982.
Turpin, Beatrice, *Le Jeu de la langue chez Saussure*, thèse de 3e cycle, Université de Paris X.
Wunderli, Peter, *Ferdinand de Saussure und die Anagramme*, Niemeyer, Tübingen 1972.

BIBLIOGRAPHY TO PART ONE

Commentaries on Saussure

Amacker, René, *Linguistique saussurienne*, Droz, Geneva 1975.

Cahiers Ferdinand de Saussure, Geneva 1941, passim.

Calvet, Louis-Jean, *Pour et contre Saussure*, Payot, Paris 1975.

Chiss, Jean-Louis, 'Synchronie/diachronie: méthodologie et théorie en linguistique', *Langages* 49, 1978.

Chomsky, Noam, *Current Issues in Linguistic Theory*, Mouton, The Hague 1964.

——, *Aspects of the Theory of Syntax*, MIT Press, Cambridge (Mass.) 1965.

Culler, Jonathan, *Saussure*, Fontana, Glasgow 1976.

Engler, Rudolf, 'Théorie et critique d'un principe saussurien: l'arbitraire du signe', *Cahiers Ferdinand de Saussure* 19, 1962.

——, *Lexique de la terminologie saussurienne*, Spectrum, Utrecht and Anvers 1968.

Haroche, Claudine, Henry, Paul, and Pêcheux, Michel, 'La Sémantique et la coupure saussurienne', *Langages* 24, 1971.

Milner, Jean-Claude, 'Réflexions sur l'arbitraire du signe', *Ornicar?* 5, 1975.

——, *L'Amour de la langue*, Seuil, Paris 1978.

Mounin, Georges, *Saussure ou le structuralisme sans le savoir*, Seghers, Paris 1968.

Normand, Claudine, 'Propositions et notes en vue d'une lecture de F. de Saussure', *La Pensée* 154, 1970.

——, 'L'Arbitraire du signe comme phénomène de déplacement', *Dialectiques* 1, 1973.

——, 'Langue/parole: constitution et enjeu d'une opposition', *Langages* 49, 1978.

Slakta, Denis, 'Esquisse d'une théorie lexico-sémantique: pour une analyse d'un texte politique', *Langages* 23, 1971.

Accessible works on Saussurian linguistics and its history

Arrivé, Michel, Gadet, Françoise, and Galmiche, Michel, *La Grammaire d'aujourd'hui*, Flammarion, Paris 1986 (dictionary of grammatical and linguistic terms).

Benveniste, Emile, *Problèmes de linguistique générale*, Gallimard, Paris 1966.

Chiss, Jean-Louis, Filliolet, Jacques, and Maingueneau, Dominique, *Initiation à la linguistique structurale*, two volumes, Hachette, Paris 1977–78.

Ducrot, Oswald, 'Le Structuralisme en linguistique', *Qu-est-ce que le structuralisme?*, Seuil, Paris 1968.

——, and Todorov, Tzvetan, *Encyclopedic Dictionary of the Sciences of Language*, Basil Blackwell, Oxford 1981.

Lepschy, Giulio, *A Survey of Structural Linguistics*, André Deutsch, London 1982.

Mounin, Georges, *La Linguistique du XXe siècle*, Presses Universitaires de France, Paris 1972 (a chapter on each of the principal linguists of the twentieth century).

SAUSSURE AND CONTEMPORARY CULTURE

Normand, Claudine, *et al.*, *Avant Saussure*, Editions Complexe, Brussels 1978 (presentation with commentaries of texts from the period 1875–1924).

2

AN IMAGINARY
HERITAGE

The Swiss linguist Ferdinand de Saussure died in 1913, leaving behind a relatively limited published oeuvre given an academic career spanning thirty years. Moreover, due to their recondite subject-matter and specialist methodology, his sparse works remain inaccessible to a wider public.

A few decades later, Saussure's name was to be among the most frequently cited not only in linguistics, but also in the human sciences and philosophy. This is because, on the basis of the CGL, he is generally regarded as the founder of 'structuralism'.

To take only one of the many examples of this putative genealogy, in the introduction to *Untying the Text: A Poststructuralist Reader*, the following definition of structuralism is offered: 'Structuralism as a proper name includes a number of diverse practices across different disciplines in the human sciences. What they all have in common is a use of Saussurian linguistics.'[1] Such formulations call for some scrutiny of their employment of the terms 'Saussurian linguistics' (Saussure's linguistics, or linguistics which claims inspiration from his principles?) and 'use' (application of a method? analogy of objects?). They also indicate the need to examine what occurred between 1916 and the 1960s to make such an association possible.

Our intention is to explore the path opened in 1916 with the publication of a book whose sole ambition (as declared by Saussure in his teaching and repeated by his editors) was one of clarification in a discipline only just beginning to win academic respectability – a path which was to lead, fifty years later, to supposed paternity of an important scientific and philosophical current.

The CGL's primary destiny was gradually to inspire the linguistic current which became 'structural linguistics', with all the discussions, reservations, reformulations, exclusions, incomprehension, etc., that the emergence of a particularly militant new theory in a field of knowledge can entail. This period extends from the 1920s to the 1960s, and our first task will be to study the transition from the CGL to structural linguistics.

The end of this phase witnessed the emergence of what has been called 'generalized structuralism', symbolized by a series of names: Claude Lévi-Strauss, Roland Barthes, Jacques Lacan, Michel Foucault, and a few less well known or less representative figures. 'Structuralism in the human sciences' developed to the frequent astonishment of structuralist linguists themselves, for it occurred at a time when their discipline was in crisis. As Benveniste was to remark: 'For a linguist accustomed to practice linguistic work and who, like me, was interested in structuralism early on, it is surprising to witness the vogue for this doctrine, ill understood and discovered belatedly, at a time when structuralism in linguistics is already out-moded for some people.'[2]

In effect two breaches were made in the edifice of structural linguistics in the 1960s: one resulting from the problematizations effected by a linguistic system – generative grammar – which shared some of its postulates; the other provoked by the problematics of enunciation, discourse, and the speaking subject. If 'Saussurian linguistics' still constitutes a model, it is certainly not as the strict application of a method, but in a broader and less rigorous sense.

Our work will conclude by investigating which aspects, assimilations and reformulations made the extension of structuralism from linguistics to the human sciences possible.

1. The editorial fortunes of the CGL

In the original French the CGL has had a prosperous history, going through numerous reprints, followed by the establishment

of a critical edition. Moreover, it has been translated into many
languages: Japanese (1928), German (1931), Russian (1933),
Spanish (1945), English (US, 1959), Polish (1961), Italian
(1967), Hungarian (1967), Serbo-Croat (1969), Swedish
(1970), Portuguese (1971), Vietnamese (1973), Korean (1975),
Turkish (1976), Albanian (1977), Greek (1979), Chinese (1980)
and English again (UK, 1983).

The Italian translation by Tullio de Mauro contains a vast
critical apparatus as well as the only significant biographical
note available. Some of the translations have gone through
several editions, and even wholesale restructuring to take
account of the critical labours of Godel, Engler and de Mauro.
In Japan, for example, a revised version of the 1928 translation
appeared in 1972 and the CGL was retranslated four years
later.

The rate of reprints and translations in different periods is
worth noting. The original text went through five editions
between 1916 and 1955, another five between 1955 and 1963,
and twenty-three between 1964 and 1985. Only five translations
appeared between 1916 and 1960, whereas there were twelve
between 1960 and 1980. This imbalance cannot be explained
by what occurred in linguistics in the 1960s, but by the apogee
of generalized structuralism. With its repeated references to
Saussure, the latter justified intense interest in a text that
remained as difficult as ever, and which had perhaps been
rendered even more difficult by what, thanks to Godel's work,
was known after 1957 about its relationship to the sources from
which it was constructed.

2. The immediate reception: from a narrow circle to the
inception of circles

The future bestseller started modestly enough in the 1920s: it
was the subject of a limited number of generally critical reviews.
Authors other than the editors only really began to incorporate
it into their theoretical work fifteen years after publication.

2.1 Reviews on publication

Initial reviews were few in number – something partially explained by its publication at the height of the First World War. Nevertheless, some of these were written by the great names in contemporary linguistics. Tullio de Mauro lists fifteen for the first edition (including Grammont, Jespersen, Meillet, Schuchardt, Séchehaye and Terracini) and seven for the second of 1922 (including Marouzeau and Uhlenbeck).

Rereading them today, one is struck by the fact that they in no way anticipate the apparent future consensus on the CGL in the 1950s. Moreover, it is noticeable that the concepts which attract comment are not always those now generally regarded as the most novel.

We shall limit ourselves to two extreme examples: the review by Meillet – an example of total incomprehension, albeit sympathetic; and that by Séchehaye – an enthusiastic defender, probably one of the few to grasp the work's significance from the outset.

Antoine Meillet followed some of Saussure's courses in Paris and was the epistolary confidante of his linguistic disarray. As virtually the sole reviewer for the *Bulletin de la Société de Linguistique*, in 1916 Meillet was already a master of French linguistics. It is therefore worth examining which Saussurian themes he focused upon in the two reviews he wrote in 1916 (for the *Bulletin*) and 1917 (for the *Revue critique de Philologie et d'Histoire*).

Positively received were *langue/parole* (a notion which 'should become established') and synchrony/diachrony (an opposition stressed at length by this unrepentant comparatist). Then come the 'objections': to the flimsiness evinced by the restricted space allocated to *parole*, predominantly presented by Meillet in a perspective of linguistic change (thereby revealing that he could not accept either synchrony or the system). He declares: 'A language that is actually spoken can be described only if the differences resulting from the diversity of social conditions and the whole structure of the society in question are taken into account'.[3] This represents Meillet's own position – one quite irreconcilable with Saussure's. The review concludes with a tribute to his 'elegant and concise etymological demonstration':

114

for Meillet Saussure remains a great comparatist (the Saussure of the *Mémoire*), and the CGL cannot compensate for his unfinished work.

The opposite extreme is represented by Séchehaye, admittedly one of the editors of the CGL. His review – actually a thirty-page article – appeared in the *Revue Philosophique* in 1917.[4]

Underlining Saussure's rupture with the comparatists and neogrammarians, Séchehaye stresses the philosophical dimension of his work: his aim was 'to think the object of linguistics in its specificity vis-à-vis all the other objects of science'. But Séchehaye is not content to list the dichotomies. He proposes a grid for their organization according to seven theses: 1) *langue/parole*; 2) *langue* as semiological system; 3) but a particular semiology, founded on values; 4) values are relative and differential; 5) change eludes the action of speakers; 6) synchrony/diachrony; 7) synchrony as a fortuitous state. He insists at length on something frequently missing from other reviews – the set of value – difference – opposition – relative arbitrariness. His conclusion offers a synthesis of Saussure's thought: 'the science of *langue* is a science of values'.

Although a somewhat narrow way of gauging the reception given to Saussurian theory, examination of the reviews presents us with an image of a restricted, slow and fragmentary diffusion. With a few exceptions, only some of the antinomies are assimilated, without any concern for the theoretical whole; whilst anything that does not directly correspond to a familiar and approved framework is excluded. This dispersion represents a pattern which we shall frequently encounter.

2.2 The world of linguistics between the wars

It is not our intention to offer a history of linguistics, but simply to indicate those factors indispensable to an understanding of the process which, in the 1920s and 1930s, was to lead to an apparent consensus on structural linguistics.

Prior to the First World War linguistics was essentially a German discipline (the comparatists and neogrammarians). Immediately afterwards, francophone and Russian scholars took over. A symbolically significant moment in the new configur-

ation was the first International Congress of Linguists at The
Hague in 1928. In response to the questions tabled for debate
by the organizers, one proposition was presented by the
Russians Jakobson, Karcevskij and Trubetzkoy, another by the
Genevans Bally and Séchehaye. Both used Saussurian theory to
describe *langue* as a system. Indeed, sufficient common ground
existed for it to be possible to merge them into a single text,
which appears in the proceedings.

Like Saussure, Bally and Séchehaye were Swiss and not
French. At this stage, under the influence of Meillet, France
remained aloof from the new current. Its reputation for being
the first country to assimilate Saussure's thought (de Mauro)
was only vindicated in the 1930s with Martinet, Benveniste and
Tesnière, all of whom were more or less linked to the Prague
Circle.

Meillet and Grammont had been taught by Saussure himself
but by the Saussure of 1880–90, who may have anticipated
the later Saussure in some respects, but was nonetheless a
comparatist. Moreover, the fact that they acknowledged a debt
to him does not mean that they were 'Saussurians'; and some
of Meillet's pupils (like Vendryès) can be characterized as pre-
Saussurians. Although indirect, Saussure's influence on
Benveniste was more decisive (Benveniste still regarded him as
primarily a comparatist in the 1930s, but soon recognized the
rupture he had effected). This was also true of Martinet (who
rarely referred to Saussure in his work, but then always
positively).

The case of Russia is quite distinct. Saussure's ideas spread
very quickly and decisively, thanks doubtless to theoretical
convergences with the formalism current in Moscow (the
Moscow Linguistic Circle) and Saint Petersburg (*Opojaz*, the
Society for the Study of Poetic Language). This was due to
Karcevskij, who had attended some of Saussure's courses in
Geneva and always maintained his contacts with the Genevans
whilst being linked to Jakobson and Trubetzkoy through the
Moscow Circle.

However, the years 1930–50 were marked by a violent anti-
formalism, whether among the official adherents of Marrism
who oscillated between liquidation and violent criticism of

Saussurian theory, or certain members of Bakhtin's circle, like Voloshinov. Formalist theses were to be more or less officially rehabilitated after Stalin's 'clarification' in 1950 (in *Marxism and Linguistics*), which reduced Marrist excesses to much ado about nothing. But the debate between supporters of historicist methods and proponents of structuralism, which was defended by such linguists as Saumjan, Revzin, Ivanov and Mel'cuk, remained bitter. An example of a particularly violent attack, directed against Saussure as a representative of 'modernism', is Abaiev's article, 'Modernism and the Dehumanization of Linguistics' (1965), in which Saussure and his followers were condemned for their 'anti-humanism', formalism and abstraction, and (as a consequence of the absence of man) for practising a 'linguistics in the void'.[5]

The barriers to the new linguistic theory in German-speaking countries were very strong: the neogrammarian school was well-established and well-organized, and continued to produce far from negligible work. Criticisms of certain Saussurian notions (e.g., Walter von Wartburg on synchrony/diachrony) and assertions that they contained nothing new (relative to Georg von de Gabelentz, Kruszewski and Baudouin de Courtenay, for example) aside, Trier was one of the few to appreciate that his conception of semantic fields owed something to Saussure's teaching.

2.3 From one circle to another

'a doctrine . . . of which the names of Ferdinand de Saussure and Roman Jakobson will stand for the dawn and its present-day culmination, not forgetting that the pilot science of structuralism in the West has its roots in Russia, where formalism first flourished.'[6] Thus Lacan sums up the link between Saussure and the linguist who did most to make him known – the link between what might be called the two sources of structuralism: Geneva and Moscow.

The phase which began in the 1920s, and which was later held to mark the rise of structuralism, took the form of a circulation of men and ideas, which might be symbolized by the term 'circle': *krouzek, krouzek, kreds, cercle, circle, circolo*. . .

Prior to the creation of the Moscow Linguistic Circle (1915),

117

the term was not generally applied to academic societies. It had been used in Russia since the nineteenth century to refer to gatherings of friends in the literary and philosophical world; this was how Baudouin de Courtenay described his regular meetings with collaborators and students at Kazan in the years 1880–90.

The kind of flexible organization inaugurated by the Moscow Linguistic Circle, which transcended the university framework and institutional constraints, adopted the title of Circle in assigning itself 'the task of elucidating the linguistic problems of ordinary language and poetic language, as well as questions of folk traditions and ethnology.'[6] It was in the works of the Moscow Circle that the term 'structural laws', identified in linguistics and poetics, first appeared.

Ten years later, the Prague linguists signalled their affinity with this pioneering research by adopting the name of Prague Linguistic Circle, an organization created on 16 October 1926. From 1929 onwards they published the *Travaux du Cercle Linguistique de Prague* (PLK).

In their turn the Copenhagen linguists followed the example of Prague. As Jakobson puts it: 'Inspired by the vigorous participation of PLK at the International Congress of Linguists at Geneva, Danish linguists founded the *Cercle Linguistique de Copenhague* in September 1931. Active cooperation and mutual discussions linked both circles'.[7] The Circle equipped itself with a journal, the *Travaux du Cercle Linguistique de Copenhague*, in 1936, and in 1939 established the review *Acta Linguistica*, designed to seal the collaboration of the Prague and Copenhagen Circles, but confined by political events to Denmark. Both Hjelmslev and Jakobson were members of the editorial committee and it featured the work of all those in Europe who identified with the Saussurian tradition, in particular Benveniste and Trubetzkoy.

On 30 October 1934 the Linguistic Circle of New York was set up by the intellectuals who had created the Ecole Libre des Hautes Etudes de New York and linguists from Columbia University. In 1945 it founded a review, *Word*, to consolidate 'the intimate cooperation between American and European linguists of different schools' and to avoid scientific isolationism,

118

with Jakobson on the editoral committee. Its multi-disciplinary outlook already anticipates structuralism's expansion beyond linguistics: 'With the title WORD we intend to emphasize the multiform natural structure of linguistic reality and the necessity for studying language in all the fullness of its various functions and relations.'[8] Levi-Strauss' presence among the authors of this first number, with an article on the parallel applications of structural analysis in linguistics and anthropology, is emblematic.

The term 'circle' spread in numerous countries, and circles less famous than the four cited here were created. That it marked an era and had significant implications is suggested by Jakobson's addition of a note when reprinting an article of 1965 in his *Selected Writings*. Explaining the change of name of the Linguistic Circle of New York to the International Linguistic Association, its President declared on 9 November 1968: 'Ours is no longer a circle. Dictionaries usually define circle as "a pleasant little group". Furthermore, the relationship that could have been drawn years ago between our organisation and the circles of Prague, Copenhagen and Paris no longer exists.'[9] This may be taken to mark the end of linguistic structuralism's ascendancy.

3. The structuralist schools

There is obviously no direct line of descent leading from Saussure to linguistic structuralism; it was constituted through the creation of a number of linguistic schools. We are now going to examine how they situated themselves in relation to him, successively reviewing the Prague Circle, glossematics (the Copenhagen Circle), the Geneva School, American distributionalism and generative grammar.

This is not to suggest that the various schools were influenced by Saussure in identical fashion. Only the first three explicitly declared themselves his heirs. Nevertheless, all five contain certain features which can be characterized as 'structuralist'. Moreover, if only negatively, they each played a role in the generalization of structuralism to the human sciences.

119

3.1 The Prague Circle and its French extensions

The term 'structuralism' originated with the Prague Circle, and was chosen to distinguish it from the formalism of the Moscow Circle: 'It [the Circle] designated itself as structuralism, its basic concept being structure conceived as a dynamic ensemble', writes Mukařovský.[10]

The linguists of the Prague Circle always claimed to draw their inspiration from Saussure (for instance at the Hague Congress). But the CGL was far from being the only influence upon them. They were equally and doubtless more profoundly influenced by Russian Formalism, Husserl's phenomenology, Brentano's philosophy, and by the psychology of *Gestalt* and Bühler, from which they borrowed the very term 'structure'. Furthermore, their conception of structure owes something to the mathematical sense of the term. The scientific links maintained by the Prague Circle were many and various (e.g., the Vienna Circle), and illustrious visitors were welcomed, including Husserl and Carnap in 1935.

The Circle was created in 1926 by the Czechs Mathesius, Mukařovský, and Vachek and the Russian immigrants Trubetzkoy, Jakobson and Karcevskij. But the symbolic founding act, in 1929, was the drafting of nine programmatic theses in French and Czech, the first three of which were general points about language, the remaining six proposals for the renovation of Slav studies.

The first thesis sets out some general principles regarding *langue*. It is entitled 'problems of method resulting from the conception of *langue* as a functional system. . .'; to which the first sub-title adds: 'conception of *langue* as a *functional* system' (my emphasis). The second sub-title, 'Tasks of the synchronic method', immediately introduces a distance vis-à-vis Saussure: 'one should not erect insurmountable barriers between the synchronic and diachronic methods, as does the Geneva School'.[11]

It might be said that all of Prague's ambivalence towards the Saussurian heritage can be found in this first thesis. The conception of *langue* as a system appears to be directly inherited from Saussure. But the adjective 'functional' posits a teleology totally foreign to him and inspired by Bühler's functions ('*langue* is a system of means of expressions appropriate to an end', the first thesis further asserts).

This brings us back to the definition of the system: doesn't linking it to a function entail a conception which owes more to Husserl (the intentional nature of consciousness) than Saussure? The linguist's methodology appeals to the direct awareness of the speaker, to his or her capacity for introspection. This is where the intuition of Husserl's subject and Saussure's synchrony can coalesce: introspection as a philosophical product of the subject's consciousness does not yield a practice very different from the analysis inferred from awareness of Saussurian *langue*.

The Prague Circle was equally concerned with poetry and phonology, an interesting combination which Milner characterizes thus: 'what is so impressive about Jakobson is that he recognized what I call the "the point of poetry" in an instance which is defined as possessing no signification: the phoneme'.[12]

From a linguistic perspective, functionalism attained its best results in the field of phonology, in particular with Trubetzkoy's *Grundzüge der Phonologie* (1939). A sound is not a bearer of signification in itself; yet it participates in signification, in so far as it is not another sound. Thus if the word *ton* ('tone') differs from *don* ('gift'), it is by virtue of the difference between *t* and *d*, which are distinctive in French (sufficient to distinguish one word from another). The recourse to signification is minimal here, differential, and this operation, later dubbed 'commutation', directly illustrates Saussurian opposition (a unit is what distinguishes it from others).

This method appears to be a practical development of the Saussurian principle that 'in *langue* there are only differences'. The principle of pertinence supplies a protocol of abstraction which isolates those sounds that have distinctive value, and which are called 'phonemes'. On this basis a distinction will be made between phonetics (the physical science of sounds) and phonology (science of their role in the system) – a couple analogous to the Saussurian opposition between *parole* (individual realization) and *langue* (the rules of the system).

Paradoxically, however, in subsequent theoretical developments distinctiveness was to be pushed to the point where it rebounded against Saussurian analysis: the distinctive features, ultimate constituents of the phoneme (in our example *ton/don*, the distinctive feature permitting the opposition between *t* and *d* is sonority), are no longer of the order of linearity; they are joined together into a single segment.

With these two reservations – the appeal to function and the extension of analysis to distinctive features – the method of distinctiveness owes a lot to Saussure, as is evident from the contrast with the definition proposed by Baudouin de Courtenay, a precursor for whom the phoneme remains dependent upon the speaker's perception (the phoneme is a 'psychological equivalent of the sound'). The formulations introduced by the Prague Circle were to be progressively detached from any psychologistic connections (the phoneme as representation of a sound) and become specifically linguistic.

The Prague Circle's other great creative achievement was in comparative linguistics, where Jakobson, Trubetzkoy and the Pole Kurilowicz made significant contributions. The intersection of the domains of phonology and comparative linguistics also led to the emergence of a purely functionalist extension in France, with the work of André Martinet, who was close to the Circle, yet pursued his own problematic. For Martinet phonetic facts are to be analysed in respect of the linguistic function performed by phonic differences. Language must satisfy the demands of communication (differentiation), but at the same time obey the tendency towards economy of effort (the fewest possible units of the maximum similarity) – contradictory tendencies within which each language finds its own equilibrium, activated in an organization as a 'double articulation' (involving monemes and phonemes).

For both the Prague Circle and Martinet, the fact that the theory of *langue* is tributary to communication entails the emergence of a blockage between the non-signifying level and signifying levels. Whilst the tie-up between functional and distinctive on the phonological level is scarcely surprising, it is by no means obvious that it will obtain at the syntactical and semantic levels.

The rare attempts later made by functionalists outside Prague to extend the theory into the domain of syntax plainly reveal its limitations. One exception is Jakobson's study of the morphology of the Russian verb.[13] Its opposition between marked and unmarked represents an interesting theoretical departure. But this is probably because it is concerned with morphology. When Martinet sought to construct a functional syntax, he had recourse to quite different analytical principles from those current in phonology. A division into predicate and complements, for example, cannot be established by means of commutation. Any relationship with the Saussurian principle of difference has disappeared.

In the field of semantics Prieto likewise attempted an analysis in terms homologous to those of phonology, seeking, by varying the message, to establish the list of distinctive elements. But he too necessarily reverted to principles other than formal commutation to describe semantic organization: in principle contrastive features recall the differential analysis of distinctive features, but they do not possess the same exacting rigour.

From the Prague linguists to Martinet and Prieto, a kind of drift is evident, taking us further and further from Saussure. It only remains to repeat our original question: is the Prague Circle a direct descendant of Saussure? To answer it, we must decide what weight to accord the arguments for and against. Among the arguments for is the fact that opposition is undoubtedly an extension of the Saussurian principle of difference and a utilization of value. One might even say that the Prague Circle discovered in phonology *the* object which imparts substance to a principle that remains abstract in Saussure. But there are also arguments against: the Prague School only employs the principle of distinctiveness by means of two non-Saussurian characteristics. The first is the role allotted to communication (a term which does not figure in the CGL), the second the functional nature of the finality of language. Despite Martinet's attempts to establish that teleologism was not indispensable to Prague phonology, it would appear that this involves a mode of thought quite foreign to Saussure's own conception (see above pp. 50–1).

3.2 Glossematics (the Copenhagen Circle)

A school was established around the Danish linguists Hjelmslev, Brøndal and Uldall, which from 1931 was organized into the

Linguistic Circle of Copenhagen and proclaimed itself a continuator (indeed the true continuator) of Saussure. This opinion is shared by Greimas, who writes in his preface to the French translation of *Language* (1966) that Hjelmslev is 'the true, perhaps the only continuator of Saussure, able to make his intuitions explicit and endow them with a definitive form'.[14]

Glossematics, and its best-known exponent Hjelmslev, represent a strange case in linguistics. Hjelmslev is little read, rarely referred to positively, and would appear to hold scant appeal for linguists, who tend to 'see in him a useless and/or caricatural double of Saussure'.[15] Yet the terms in which he reformulated Saussurian concepts are frequently those adopted, sometimes without their users knowing it, to expound Saussurian theory – as if his conceptual displacements were of no consequence. This idea of a smooth continuation, even a harmonious development, is taken up by Ruwet in an assessment of 'general linguistics today', where he speaks of the fundamental concepts of structural linguistics 'stated by Saussure and elaborated by Hjelmslev'.[16]

Hjelmslev considered his work sufficiently innovatory to warrant a new designation: glossematics. Whilst acknowledging a 'profound debt' to Saussure, he declared himself a theoretical innovator. Glossematics constitutes a rigorous problematic, an axiomatized theory – a genuinely autonomous linguistics (a 'linguistic' or 'immanent' linguistics as it came to be called).

The basic postulate is that to every sequence there corresponds an underlying structure which may be described with a limited number of premises and theorems. The sequence, which is observable, is termed 'process'; it can be analysed into elements arranged in classes, an inventory of whose potential combinations is possible. The underlying structure, extracted by abstraction, is the system. This conception, reminiscent of the Saussurian system, has led some commentators to invoke Chomsky's 'deep structures'. We prefer to speak of formalized writing, the result of what Hjelmslev described as an 'empirical' approach (whose requirements are a non-contradictory, exhaustive and simple theoretical form), as opposed to an inductive procedure.

Hjelmslev establishes his 'stratification of language' by articulating two Saussurian theses:

– *langue* is form, not substance;

– every language is both 'expression' and 'content'.

The first thesis is manifestly impeccably Saussurian. It leads to the idea of system, for the form of a language constitutes an original division [*découpage*] peculiar to that language.

As to the second, it contains terms absent from Saussure – reformulations of signifier (expression) and signified (content). What are the implications of this displacement? Hjelmslev rules out any critique in terms of banalization ('the terms "expression" and "content" have been selected according to ordinary usage and are completely arbitrary'). In Saussure the bond between the two propositions is the theory of the sign. Hjelmslev retains the sign, but redefines it at the interface of the four concepts form/substance, content and expression: 'The sign is, then – paradoxical as it may seem – a sign for a content-substance and a sign for an expression-substance.'[17]

Both sides of the sign are amenable to a structural analysis – whence the importance of commutation, a fundamental relation which is the key to understanding languages. Commutation is thus of much greater import than in the Prague Circle, where it is only employed for the level of expression.

Relative to Saussure, glossematics operates a displacement of the object of linguistics, at once restricting and expanding it. It is restricted to the extent that, linguistics being the science of form, domains related to substance (e.g., phonematics, graphematics and semantics) are excluded. But it simultaneously undergoes an expansion, for the specificity of articulated languages is defined within a typology of sign systems. The multifunctional character of languages (any language can serve any end), which makes possible an infinity of significations (and its corollary, translatability), serves to distinguish two types of languages: restricted or 'conformal' languages, which exhibit a biunivocal correspondence between expression and content; and all-purpose or 'non-conformal' languages (natural languages, principally, and possibly dreams), which possess two different forms for content and expression. Notwithstanding the differences, the two types share features which can be regarded as THE basic structure of language:

– two sides (expressed in the relationship between expression and content);

– opposition between process and underlying system;

– relation of denotation – the way in which the units of content and the units of expression are inter-linked;

– non-conformity between the analysis of expression and the analysis of content.

The emphasis on the similarities between restricted systems and specifically linguistic systems explains why Hjelmslev has had more influence in semiotics than in linguistics proper; his true heirs are Greimas and the Barthes of *Elements of Semiology* (1964). The semiotician Rastier finds consolation for this lack of linguistic posterity: 'His influence is felt in another way: his theory of language – glossematics – possesses a significance transcending linguistics and can contribute to the foundation of a general semiotics'.[18]

The Prague linguists can be reproached for the heterogeneity of their philosophical references. Nothing of the sort applies to Hjelmslev, whose only references are to logicians – Carnap, Whitehead, Russell and Tarski.

Glossematics went through several phases, and the article 'The Stratification of Langage' partially calls into question the equilibrium postulated by the *Prolegomena* (1943). Indeed, Hjelmslev belatedly sought to reintegrate the referent into language, to 'semiotize right up to that lump of rebel substance known as the "physical level" '.[19] This is a strange enterprise, and we may wonder whether linguistics as constituted by Saussure does not get bogged down in it. Attuned to the pre-Saussurian regression, Meschonnic's characterization of Hjelmslev as 'Saussure's greatest posthumous misfortune'[20] is understandable. Without necessarily going that far, it can be said that Hjelmslev introduces a closure into Saussurianism by taking certain principles to extremes: contrary to Saussure's system, Hjelmslev's is without residue, without flaw, without infinity.

3.3 The Geneva School

It would be wrong to imagine that the Saussurian heritage was naturalized to any great extent in Switzerland, and the title 'Geneva School', criticized by the very people thought to belong to it, in fact refers to isolated personalities rather than a real current.

Three periods can be distinguished in the Swiss reception of Saussurianism:

– from 1916 to the end of the Second World War, when, given the polemics over Saussure's main concepts (e.g., Dorozewski against the phoneme, Wartburg against synchrony/diachrony, Buyssens on the sign), Bally and Séchehaye (the latter probably closer to the Saussurian project) felt themselves charged with a defensive mission. *Cahiers Ferdinand de Saussure* was created to this end in 1941.

– after 1945, as Saussure's teaching began to be taken up by structuralism (essentially the Prague and Copenhagen Schools), work was directed to a deeper understanding of its coherence and systematicity.

– after the publication of the *Sources* and the Second Course in 1957 (both by Godel), a 'second Saussurian generation' made its appearance (Frei, Burger, Godel, Engler, and the Argentinian Prieto, who taught at Geneva). The tone became less apologetic and the research undertaken modified the traditional image of the CGL.

However, it is from the first period that Henri Frei's *La grammaire des fautes* (1929) dates – an important study scarcely known outside the ranks of sociolinguists and specialists working on popular idiom. In many ways, it is worthy of inclusion in a list of structuralist works directly heir to Saussure.

Frei started out from a hypothesis on the role of 'errors' in identifying or repairing the deficits of the correct system. From a functionalist perspective (which he contrasted to Saussure's 'normative' attitude), he viewed the evolution of languages as governed by a small number of basic and constant linguistic requirements: assimilation and its counter-part, differentiation, or a tendency to clarity; economy, manifested syntagmatically in brevity and associatively in invariability; expressivity, which counteracts semantic wear and tear. These prerequisites, all of which have memorial manifestations (associative relations) and discursive manifestations (syntagmatic relations), can coincide or conflict, producing stability or instability in linguistic systems.

Frei's theoretical position is reminiscent of aspects of the Prague Circle or Martinet. But his activation of memory and discourse at all levels may be said to constitute an interesting application of the two Saussurian axes.

3.4 American structuralism, or distributionalism, or the Yale School

Between 1920 and 1940 American linguistics was dominated by Bloomfield. In 1924 he gave the CGL a very favourable review. But in his major work, *Language* (1933), Saussure's name only appears once, and then in a purely historical connection. The definitive character of this work explains the relative lack of interest in Saussure's œuvre on the part of the Americans: it is comprehensive, a simultaneously theoretical and empirical summa which probably corresponded more to their expectations.

It was in this period of ignorance of Saussure that one of the best overall studies of the CGL appeared, Wells' 'De Saussure's System of Linguistics' (1947), which seeks to identify its theoretical coherence. Indeed, so subtle was Wells' reading that it pinpointed some of the text's obscurities – for example, in connection with value (the 'and that is why' of p. 113) which we have seen (p. 57) to be an interpolation by the editors. Ten years before Godel, Wells was able to detect, by an internal reading, the discrepancy in the text which 'makes it sound as if arbitrariness resulted from the nature of value; but this contravenes de Saussure's whole teaching, and is merely careless wording'.[21]

Derived from the work of Bloomfield and developed by Wells and Harris, distributionalism dominated American linguistics until the mid-1950s – the precise period when linguistic structuralism was developing in Europe. Its adherents never referred to Saussure. Even so, aspects of it recall European structuralism, and we may speak of a convergence of analyses if not a filiation (the divergences are scarcely insignificant).

Distributionalism's starting-point is behaviourist psychology, the idea being that human behaviour can be completely explained on the basis of the situations in which it occurs. Accordingly, a mechanistic interpretation of speech can be proposed. Hence the linguist's sole recourse is to description, excluding any study of meaning (by definition unobservable).

Starting from a corpus comprising a set of utterances as received (thus without resort to any opposition of the kind *langue/parole*), the linguist locates regularities, appealing, not to function or signification, but exclusively to the environments that define a unit's 'distribution'. Distributionalism is thus classificatory rather than explanatory. Its single procedure makes it possible to conceive of language as homogeneous from the phoneme to the sentence, with no discrepancies between the levels (thus avoiding the blockage involved in functionalism).

Distributionalism proceeds from these definitions to two types of activity:

– a decomposition of utterances into immediate constituents, which reveals the hierarchical construction of the minimal units in immediate constituents;

– a classification of the constituents into distributional classes. These two levels characterize the distributional structure of language.

The essential point upon which distributionalism and Saussurianism diverge concerns the determination of the units. Never simply given for Saussure, they are the object of a prior knowledge in distributional study. The analysis into immediate constituents, which appears to resolve this difficulty, encounters two problems: delimitation of units smaller than the word and identification of occurrences of the same unit.

If distributionalism can be linked to structuralism, it is to the glossematic version: they share the characterization of languages by a set of combinatory regularities. Two points of divergence remain, however:

– glossematics is concerned with both expression and content, whereas distributionalism excludes meaning;

– distributionalism is completely bound up with the linearity of the signifier – a restriction not imposed by glossematics (as its study of content demonstrates).

Just as glossematics is opposed to the Prague Circle on the

role of function, distributionalism is opposed to Pike's tagmemics, which distinguishes between exclusive concentration on spatio-temporal characterization (attributed to the distributionalists) and the interpretation of events according to their function for the speaker (his own position).[22]

In line with Pike's typology of theories, through two tendencies in the interpretation of Saussurianism, we might contrast two fundamentally antagonistic conceptions of *langue*: one which understands it as form (Copenhagen and distributionalism) and another which conceives it as function (Prague and tagmemics).

3.5 Generative grammar

It is manifestly paradoxical to include generative grammar among the structuralist schools, in so far as its historical self-representation insists upon its rupture with the structuralist conception. However, it must be remembered that Chomsky's denunciation of 'taxonomic' methods is essentially aimed at Bloomfield's and Harris's theories, and he has remarked of European structuralism: 'personally I have learnt a lot from European structuralism, and especially from Roman Jakobson who was my teacher and a very good friend; there is no need for me to remind people how fundamental his contributions remain'.[23]

Chomsky's oeuvre can only be compared with structuralism at a general descriptive level. He demonstrates a genuine knowledge of Saussure; but was he influenced by him? It would surely be more accurate to say that he develops his own concepts and indicates, with some satisfaction, that they coincide with Saussure's.

Chomsky was formed in the Bloomfieldian school of Harris but soon distanced himself, especially from inductivism (the hypothesis that it is possible to analyse a language on the basis of a limited corpus of attested examples). Recalling Saussure he substitutes the idea of locating the underlying system – competence – which explains language acts – performance.

Rejection of the corpus as a means of access to the system represents a significant area of disagreement with distributionalism. Another such point, linked to the notion of system, is Chomsky's recognition of a dimension of knowledge about language possessed by speakers – competence – for which grammar must account (knowledge of the comparison of constructions, ambiguity, paraphrases. . .). In this respect (and ignoring certain psychological features), competence is comparable to Saussurian *langue*; Saussure and Chomsky concur on the necessity of explaining something of the way in which people speak.

Saussure was frequently and positively mentioned in Chomsky's work at the beginning of the 1960s, when the *langue/parole* distinction was recast as competence/performance (with the difference that the theory of the sentence and creativity are accorded a central role by Chomsky). At this stage there was likewise a *rapprochement* on the derivative role of semantics. Chomsky recognized Saussure as a 'pioneer of modern scientific linguistics'. His position changed with *Aspects of the Theory of Syntax*; henceforth Saussure is still cited, but credited with a 'naive view of language'.

We have seen that Chomsky's opposition to Saussure on such issues as creativity above all derived from a narrow reading of him. Whilst Saussure did not develop syntax and the sentence as much as he might have done, his conception of morpho-syntax contains the elements indispensable to any such initiative. Moreover, sufficient common ground on a conception of language according to two axes exists for Ruwet to have regarded the theory of transformations as an extension of the paradigmatic analysis to the higher levels of the utterance.[24]

Saussure and Chomsky can likewise be related at an epistemological level, in their common opposition to induction (inter-relation [*va-et-vient*] of facts and theory in Saussure, hypothetico-deductive method in Chomsky).

The subsequent evolution of generative grammar was to distance Chomsky further and further both from engagement with structuralism (soon considered outdated) and from issues that permit of any *rapprochement* with Saussure.

3.6 A discreet structuralism: Emile Benveniste
Benveniste is not really classifiable in any school, but one readily thinks of him as an exemplar of European structuralism.

Formed in the comparatist school of Meillet, interested in the work of the Prague Circle, he gradually became a structuralist

He is genuinely a structuralist, a continuator of Saussure - an exegete of the development of Saussurian concepts (cf. his reflections on the transition from the idea of 'system' to that of 'structure'); a subtle analyst of the structuralist conception of *langue*, from the definition of units to the issue of the sentence;[2] and, like Saussure, a linguist concerned with the epistemological interrogation of the object of his discipline.

But there is a totally original side to Benveniste as well, which owes nothing to Saussure (except perhaps as a consequence of a systematic project). He uncovers the dimension of the speaking subject and enunciation from within a strictly immanent structuralism by studying the distinctive behaviour of certain elements – none of which can be described without reference to the fact that a language is spoken by a subject, and is the product of an enunciation. His analysis of these so-called 'indexical' elements converges with some of the conclusions reached by the analytical philosopher Austin on performatives and by Jakobson on 'shifters'.

Two interpretations of this reintroduction of the subject into structuralist linguistics are possible, depending on whether or not the relationship between system and subject is considered to be harmonious:

– If there is continuity between the *langue*-system of signs and the *langue*-instrument of communication activated in enunciation, 'the linguistics of *langue*, system of signs, opens onto a linguistics of discourse, involving the intervention of a subject who is master of his or her *parole*, and whose presence is analysed as a system of traces'.[26] Linguistics can identify the traces of the enunciation in the product that is the utterance locate 'the formal apparatus of enunciation', as the title of an article by Benveniste puts it.

– Following Milner's interpretation,[27] this same relation will be conceived as a dramatic one: the indexical elements are 'the marks in *langue* of that which is radically other' – the index of an irreconcilable heterogeneity, the sudden emergence of a subject of desire within the system.

Jakobson's position on these phenomena is situated in a problematic of continuity: there exist in *langue* double structures which underline the fact that the combinatory of the relations between 'code' and 'message' is complex. By contrast, Lacan probably adopts the second perspective when he takes up the Benveniste of enunciation, enabling him to glimpse the impossibility of the subject within *langue*.

Benveniste taught linguists to examine the relationship between the notion of the speaking subject, previously regarded as unproblematic, and the explicitly problematic notion of the subject of the enunciation. Reflections on language benefitted greatly, and Benveniste's merit is to have induced it from the very core of structuralism.

It remains, in conclusion, to ask what allows these partially or wholly independent currents, often engendered in quite different problematics, all to be labelled 'structuralist'. Following Benveniste, and notwithstanding divergences which no attempt has been made to hide, the following common characteristics can be identified:
- the need for a descriptive approach;
- recognition of the system;
- a concern to extend the analysis to the elementary units;
- the explicit choice of procedures.

At a very general but nevertheless rigorous level, these features, although insufficient to distinguish structural linguistics from what succeeded it, do serve to differentiate it from the conception dominant in the preceding period.

4. The fate of the concepts

Sign, semiology, system, arbitrariness, *langue/parole*, synchrony/diachrony, signifier/signified, and occasionally value... These are Saussurian terms which evoke structuralism whenever they appear – not only in linguistics, but in expanded structuralism as well. Here we shall attempt to retrace the development of each concept or group of concepts – the way in which they have been received and discussed, and their contemporary status in what might be called the structuralist vulgate.

133

From the standpoint of the totality of Saussurian theory, examination of the concepts in isolation or even in groups is hardly adequate. For this is yet again to treat them as discrete entities (a remark of Engler's when surveying the destiny of the antinomies comes to mind: 'incapable of deceiving Saussure in his lifetime, words have had the upper hand after his death').[28] But ultimately it is the only way to establish that, contrary to received opinion, little of Saussure's theory has been preserved in the public domain [le trésor commun] of structuralism beyond the terms themselves, and that if Saussure was transmitted to the structuralists it was not in the form of a material heritage.

4.1 The sign and related notions (signifier, signified, semiology, arbitrariness, linearity)

The plethora of publications on the sign, already highlighted by Engler in 1962[29] and continuing thereafter, should not in our view be regarded as an index of the centrality of this idea in Saussurian linguistics. When it is further noted that they are mainly the work of logicians, philosophers of language, psychologists, psycholinguists, psychoanalysts, literary theorists, semioticians, etc. – and rarely linguists – then it is clear that the sign is the anchoring-point of non-linguists' interest in Saussurian theory and structuralism. Suffice it to mention the names of Lacan, Barthes and Derrida.

Perhaps even more than the sign, the Saussurian concept which appears with greatest frequency in structuralist works is semiology – the 'science that studies the life of signs within society'. The role accorded this notion in Saussure is open to question: what space is there for it when linguistics has been assigned an object defined so rigorously via a series of exclusions? Beyond mentioning it, few linguists have made anything of semiology. However, Trubetzkoy is among them, having proposed a parallel between phonology and society which Lévi-Strauss seized upon some years later.

For non-linguists the problem is rather different. In their case the reference to semiology is productive; yet they do not always respect Saussure's own framework. Thus Barthes proposes to invert the relationship between linguistics and semiology: 'linguistics is not a part of the general science of signs, even a privileged part, it is semiology which is part of linguistics'[30] – the reason being that language alone can furnish the model for systems of communication.

Only the term 'semiology' is Saussurian, but it is frequently rivalled by 'semiotics', borrowed from the American tradition and Peirce in particular. The fact that semiology has largely become established in expanded structuralism demonstrates that, whatever the intellectual intermediaries, a Saussurian reference is undoubtedly involved (above all in Lévi-Strauss and Barthes).

The numerous articles on semiology and the sign call for two comments (possibly linked by the fact that in general it is not linguists who are concerned with the latter):

– even in the most recent of them, the CGL is much more frequently cited than the sources;

– ideas are often treated in isolation, without an overall understanding and without reference to other aspects of Saussure's constructions.

In other words, the idea is construed as entailing important consequences, yet these are not particularly developed.

Every aspect of Saussure's definition of the sign, as well as the properties attributed to it, has been subject to discussion, and it is rarely accepted in its entirety. The very notion has given rise to controversy. At what grammatical level should it be envisaged? The CGL is unclear on this point, and all sorts of solutions have been proposed: the moneme or the morpheme, the word, the syntagm, the ensemble of the sentence, or all these units at once (e.g., in Hjelmslev).

Signifier/signified: this is how the Saussurian sign, in its very constitution, expresses the fact that *langue* establishes a relation between something physically present (the signifier) and something absent (meaning, the signified) – a connection no linguist can afford to ignore. But signifier/signified is only one version of this idea, and the different schools have reacted to it in various ways – adopting it, in line with Saussure; reformulating it as expression and content, in the case of Hjelmslev; relegating and then rehabilitating it at the point of grammar's organization into levels, in the case of Chomsky.

The most celebrated reappropriation of the sign, still analysed

135

in terms of signifier and signified, is Lacan's. He interprets it according to the schema S/s, introduced with remarkable understatement: 'This sign should be attributed to Ferdinand de Saussure although it is not found in exactly this form in any of the numerous schemas ... in the printed version of his lectures'.[31] Despite the attribution, the Lacanian schema is very different from Saussure's:

– in the very symbolization of the terms: capital S for the signifier and lower case s for the signified, whereas in the CGL we either find the terms in full or abbreviated as *Sign.é* [*signifié*] and *Sign.t* [*signifiant*].

– in the position each element occupies in the schema: whereas the signifier is at the base of the schema in Saussure, Lacan places it at the apex in order to symbolize the sliding of the signified under the signifier.

– in the disappearance of the ellipsis which delimits the sign in Saussure, and which appears to make of it a closed domain, in patent contradiction with what is postulated by the principle of value. Lacan thereby registers the fact that one signification always summons up another, offering a genuinely Saussurian interpretation of value.

– in the suppression of the arrows thought to represent the mutual presupposition of the two sides of the sign. It has already been noted that these arrows were added by the editors and that, rather than clarifying things, they risked facilitating the restoration of a 'nomenclative' interpretation of *langue*.

– The only feature from Saussure to survive in Lacan is the bar between the two components. But whereas it is simply posited in Saussure, unglossed, Lacan proposed to interpret it as a 'barrier resisting signification', and it is central to his theory of the signifier.

Thus we can say of Lacan's use of the Saussurian sign both that it is utterly foreign to the Saussurian conception and that it develops its implications to the full.

The first characteristic accorded the sign by Saussure in the CGL – the arbitrariness of the bond between signifier and signified – is expounded in a manner conducive to confusion, to the extent that it has been read as articulating the convention-alist philosophical position. This is Benveniste's interpretation in his celebrated article of 1939, where the necessity of the bond between signifier and signified for the speaking subject is asserted. Numerous critics have adopted it, and it is arguably the major interpretation of arbitrariness to be found in expanded structuralism.

Jakobson went so far as to conceive the bond between signifier and signified as partially motivated ('intimate connections between grammatical concepts and their phonological expression casts doubt on "the arbitrary" nature of the linguistic sign')[32] – a position he developed in a theory of 'phonetic symbolism' of particular interest to specialists in poetics.

The second property of the sign – the linearity of the signifier – has not escaped the vicissitudes of interpretation either. Propounded with great rapidity and as a self-evident fact, it has been described by Jakobson as 'nothing but a vicious circle'.[33] Distinctive or pertinent features can in part be construed as reopening the question of linearity; depending on the school, their role is more or less important, intervening exclusively on the phonic level (Prague and Martinet) or equally on the semantic level (Copenhagen and structural semantics).

In the final analysis, the essential point to be noted about the theory of the sign is the disproportion between the strong interest shown by non-linguists and the reservations of the linguists themselves. Our own explanation of this follows Milner's in *L'Amour de la langue*. Linguists consider the sign a linguistic impasse, its sole function being to relate the two orders of meaning and sound. Their only concern is that such a role is performed, whatever its modalities. For non-linguists, by contrast, the very notion of the sign connotes language; it is integral to the structuralist project. Even if they do not employ it (being concerned neither with its properties nor its theory), they cannot conceive doing without it.

4.2 Synchrony/diachrony

This dichotomy has been widely accepted – something explained by the fact that as the first Saussurian distinction to be established (it dates from 1894), it was 'in the air' both in Saussure's day and in subsequent periods.

Only the Prague Circle radically called the distinction into question. At The Hague (1928) Jakobson, Trubetzkoy and Karcevskij asserted that its elimination was a prerequisite for 'recogniz[ing] the systematic and functional nature of linguistic change'. Jakobson was never to change his mind on the issue, counterposing a 'dynamic synchrony' to the Saussurian conception. It might be thought that this involves a misunderstanding of Saussure's intentions with regard to synchrony, for the method Jakobson helped to perfect on phonology in Prague identifies structural with synchronic.

Martinet held an intermediate position between Prague and Saussure, in particular in *Economie des changements phonétiques* (1955). He criticized Saussure for getting carried away by his chess metaphor, which obscures the fact that just as nothing in *langue* exists to perform the role of the player, so there is no principle of sudden transformation from one state to another. Yet he criticized the Prague School for the teleologism of its critique, which explains change as a tendency to a more harmonious state. For Martinet the structure is certainly to be grasped at the level of synchrony (like most linguists of his time he acknowledged its primacy), but in its very organization the language-state contains the germ of the alterations it will undergo.

Faithful to the tradition of excluding any historical considerations from the description of a language-state, American linguistics adopted a radically opposed position to that of Prague. Thus Bloomfield's *Language* is constructed on classical lines: first of all descriptive linguistics, then changes. The opposition is absent from Chomsky: it does not figure in *Aspects* when generative grammar is evaluated in relation to Saussurian theory (perhaps this merely serves to signal a fundamental convergence on the primacy of the synchronic). The argument for the synchrony of a study is tacitly accepted, and arguably dictated even more strongly by the concept of competence as knowledge of a subject than by that of *langue*.

So depending on the particular theory, we find three different interpretations of the opposition between synchrony and diachrony:

– in Saussure a theoretical antinomy which, whilst positing the methodological primacy of synchrony, never ignored either the existence of change or its effects on a language-state (see, for example, his treatment of analogy as a grammatical and synchronic phenomenon, assimilable to the mechanism of *langue*);

– in the Prague Circle the attenuation of the antinomy in a 'dynamic synchrony', which does not, however, prevent the employment of a strictly synchronic method;

– in the American schools a radical opposition which leads them to speak only of synchrony.

When reference is made to incidences in structuralism of the relation between synchrony and diachrony (rendered equivalent to 'structure' and 'event'), it is generally to the third interpretation – erroneously attributed to Saussure – that commentators appeal, an example being the terms in which the debate between Marxism and structuralism is posed.

4.3 *Langage, langue, parole*

This antinomy in two parts, fundamental to the inauguration of the object of linguistics, is generally reduced to the distinction between *langue* and *parole*. That between *langage* and *langue* is rarely discussed, either because the role of *langage* is not questioned, or (in the case of semiologists) because the distinction is inadmissable, or (in the case of English speakers) because their language does not encompass it.

The distinction between *langue* and *parole* is generally accepted by linguists, the more so since it has been reinforced by the Chomskyan distinction between competence and performance. But the primacy of the study of *langue* is hardly accepted, other than by phonologists and specialists in syntax. Sociolinguists and pragmaticians deplore Saussure's lack of interest in *parole*, or suggest that an extra dimension needs to be added to him – discourse or enunciation.

We have seen that the definition of *langue/parole* is polysemic and that it is not always easy to grasp the relations between the different definitions. A symptom of the problem is the variety of glosses offered in English ('language' and 'speech' – the terms proposed by Saussure's translator, Wade Baskin – have apparently resulted neither in unanimity nor clarity). This polysemy seems to have greatly troubled linguists, and no other antinomy has been subjected to so many suggested reformulations.

Some linguists accept the dichotomous framework and limit themselves to altering its terms. Thus the Prague Circle basically adheres to the distinction, but its recasting of it as code/message in order to avoid the polysemy of the word *langue* is not without its effects on their conception of the relationship between the two domains. Reformulating *parole* as performance and *langue* as competence, Chomsky likewise maintains a dichotomy, yet modifies the place of the sentence and the conception of creativity (a 'rule-governed creativity' is accommodated in competence). This reconstruction likewise has a far from negligible effect on the relationship instituted between individual and society.

However, excepting Jakobson, who queries the necessity of the dichotomy, the proposed reformulations tend to add a term, therewith installing a trichotomy.

– Buyssens proposes to add discourse (the functional part of *parole*) between *langue* and *parole*;

– Coseriu adds norm and replaces *langue* by system (the title of his best-known work is *System, Norm and Speech* (1952)).

– Hjelmslev is predominantly concerned with the pole of *langue* and disturbed by the breadth of its reference. He therefore proposes to analyse it as comprising three elements: schema (pure form), norm (material form) and usage (set of habits). He does not touch on *parole*. Subsequently, he discarded norm, retaining the three terms schema, usage and *parole*. The fact that the majority of passages in the CGL devoted to *langue* appear to him to pertain to the schema confirms his formalized conception of Saussurian linguistics.

The *langue/parole* opposition, then, was essentially preserved, and was to be appropriated in the structuralist vulgate according to the most readily intelligible opposition in the CGL – that between social and individual.

4.4 *Langue* as a system of relations (system, value, form/substance, associative and syntagmatic relations)

Langue is a system. For the majority of commentators this is the key point of Saussurian theory – without it the idea of structuralism vanishes – and as fundamental as the idea of the sign, to which it is linked in the assertion that 'language [*langue*] is a system of signs'. However, beyond question-begging, what makes *langue* a system – value and the interplay of the associative and syntagmatic axes – is not always examined in depth.

One symptom of these concepts' significance is the change of name they undergo in the course of the history of linguistic structuralism: 'system' finds itself competing with 'structure' and 'associative' is virtually replaced outright by 'paradigmatic'. We shall now examine the implications of these terminological mutations.

Underlying the reformulation of system as structure (which is not total, however: system persists, albeit as commentary rather than concept) is the same factor as led the Prague Circle to declare itself structuralist – the influence of *Gestalt* and Husserl. It has already been suggested that this oscillation between system and structure has consequences for the conception of system – in particular, the disappearance of value from most commentaries. Value is undoubtedly a difficult concept to handle, and concrete proposals (whether in the CGL or subsequently) for a method based upon it have been scarce. Yet its absence turns system into a banality from which no-one would dissent.

Little use is made of the form/substance opposition, beyond question-begging arguments in favour of form. Such cursoriness tends to obscure the significance Saussure attached to discarding substance, on the one hand, and his dissatisfaction with the notion of form, which he put to work with value, on the other. Only Hjelmslev reserved a particular fate for form/substance, which he resumed in articulation with 'content' and 'expression'.

Hjelmslev is likewise responsible for recasting 'associative' as 'paradigmatic': 'in order to avoid the psychologism adopted in Ferdinand de Saussure's *Course* I substitute the term "paradigmatic relation" for that of "associative relation" '.[34] Psychologism? Clearly Hjelmslev connected 'association' with the associationist psychology it inevitably evoked at the time, yet this is far from being its meaning in Saussure.

There are several points to be made about this terminological change:

– 'paradigm' features in Saussure, inflectional paradigms being an example of association (CGL, p. 126). Since he had the option of using either term, Saussure obviously deliberately selected 'association', extending its meaning;

– nothing in the original meaning of the word paradigm (architectural plan, model) necessitates its restriction to the enumeration of a form's inflexions;

– Saussurian associations can play on elements irreducible to grammatical role within the system (e.g., when *clément* is associated with *enseignement*). The paradigm contains no more than the possibility of commutation within an identical syntagm, in accordance with Saussure's own procedure when he comes to the grammatical treatment of association.

Why have the vast majority of linguists followed Hjelmslev, to the point where it is now very common for 'paradigm' to figure in introductions to Saussure? By grammatical reflex? Because association leads to the swamping of grammar in a symbolic conception of *langue*? Because it is not utilizable?

Our own view is that Saussurian association, restricted in the structuralist paradigm, is probably closer to the mechanisms at work in the exercise of *parole* by a subject, yet difficult for a grammarian to use. Thus impoverishment is the price to be paid for grammar.

By contrast, in 'Two Aspects of Language and Two Types of Aphasic Disturbances' (1956)[35] – a text which attracted Lacan's attention – Jakobson employs the two axes in a way which can be seen as an extension and enrichment of the Saussurian notion. He opposes the axis of similarity (or selection – Saussure's associative axis) to that of contiguity (or combination – Saussure's syntagmatic axis), demonstrating that aphasia due to a disturbance of similarity deprives the sufferer of the faculty of finding the words to fit into a schema; whereas aphasia due to the disturbance of contiguity results in agrammatism. Recasting Saussure in the rhetorical terms of metaphor (selection) and metonymy (combination) serves to establish a parallel between the functioning of language and the functioning of dreams as described by Freud. For Jakobson symbolism pertains to the order of metaphor, whereas condensation and displacement are of the order of metonymy. Whilst modifying it slightly, Lacan was to develop this problematic.

The various linguistic schools can be characterized vis-à-vis one another in terms of their respective attitudes towards the two axes of *langue*. Only glossematics sought to accord equal significance to both. Distributionalism is essentially founded on syntagmatic analysis, in so far as it regards a language as a combinatory, identified with the actual directly observable sequence. The Prague Circle attempted to impart an intrinsic raison d'être to the associative organization of *langue*.

The tendency to privilege one axis over the other is not confined to the linguistic schools. It is also evident in the extension of the model to the human sciences. Thus, in the study of myths and folktales, Propp's syntagmatic model in his *Morphology of the Folktale* may be contrasted with the paradigmatic model employed by Lévi-Strauss under the influence of Trubetzkoy's phonology.

It can be seen that the opposition between two axes of language is extremely rich in its practical potential. For Chomsky it underpins the structuralist method founded 'on segmentation and classification'. Many other linguists base themselves on the idea, although it is not always easy to identify what derives from Saussure and what is simply common ground on *langue*. Thus the English linguist Firth opposes structure (syntagmatic arrangement) and system (paradigmatic arrangement), and Tesnière describes the antinomy between structural order (paradigmatic) and linear order (syntagmatic). Such an inversion of the meaning of the word structure is a cause for amazement – and eloquent testimony to the interpretative difficulties involved. . .

This rapid review of the fate of Saussurian concepts in their posthumous existence in linguistic and expanded structuralism suggests a mixed balance-sheet. In terms of literal ideas, whether they are adopted, reformulated, or rejected, it is frequently isolated notions or antinomies that are at stake, without consideration of the totality of Saussure's construction. Yet it is perfectly clear that there is a 'Saussure-effect' on linguists.

5. Saussure, from linguistics to the human sciences

Communication, signification, code/message, discourse... In the idiom of expanded structuralism these terms are added to those of directly Saussurian origin. They are external to Saussurianism and structural linguistics, yet pertain to language. We shall now examine what they have come to represent in structuralism in the other human sciences.

The history of structuralism might have ended with the episodes of theoretical problematization in linguistics itself. It would only remain to say that after the 1950s structuralism pursued a tranquil career, punctuated by the production of results which had already been foreseen, alongside other theories some of which profoundly challenged it. Some pronounce it dead, others living – the fate of all theories, perhaps.

Yet its history did not stop there. Towards the end of the Second World War works appeared, first in anthropology and then in the other human sciences, which, as far as public opinion is concerned, represent structuralism proper. In the space of a few years, from the most varied disciplines and problematics, such diverse figures as Claude Lévi-Strauss, Roland Barthes, Jacques Lacan, Michel Foucault, Louis Althusser and Jacques Derrida (to name but a few) found themselves labelled structuralist, although the only one to make any explicit claim to the title was Lévi-Strauss.

The structuralists in the wider sense of the word discovered Saussure in the 1940s, 50s and 60s. The traffic between linguistics and the human sciences occurred mainly through the medium of three preeminent interpretations: Jakobson (above all for Lévi-Strauss and Lacan), Hjelmslev (above all for Barthes), and Benveniste (whom Lacan describes as 'by far the greatest of the French').[36] But Barthes states that his intervention ensured that these three linguists – in the field of literary analysis at least – came to be considered resources for challenging traditional analyses: 'Jakobson's role in this offensive is well-known... From the French viewpoint, we must add the work of other linguists who contributed concepts upon which the study of discourse could profitably draw –

144

notably Hjelmslev, with the form of the content and conno-tation, and Benveniste, whose reflections on enunciation turned out to be very close to certain researches by writers themselves.'[37]

Of the three, Jakobson undoubtedly played the greatest role: his charismatic personality runs through the whole linguistic century and his impact cannot be reduced to his sometime membership of each of the linguistic schools. His centrality is incontestable because of his influence on Lévi-Strauss, who has himself been dubbed 'the father of structuralism' (in the broad sense, of course) for several reasons: his pioneering role (his first structuralist writings date from 1945); his unqualified affiliation (he is the only one readily to employ the terms 'struc-ture' and 'structural' in the titles of his works); his consistency (compare the prudence displayed in the 1970s by Barthes, who was to refer to the 'semiological adventure', therewith confiding that it was over for him); his audience (Lacan acknowledged that he had discovered Jakobson and hence Saussure via Lévi-Strauss).

5.1 The great herald of structuralism: Jakobson

'*Linguista sum; nihil linguistici a me alienum puto*'. Roman Jakobson was fond of defining himself with this variation on Terence's celebrated dictum. The antithesis of the Saussurian attempt to furnish linguistics with a narrow and rigorous object, he was an especially appropriate relay-point for the diffusion of Saussurian themes, between the demands of structural linguis-tics and those of the other human sciences.

Present throughout our study, Jakobson stands out among linguists in several respects:

– his internationalism. His life took him from Moscow to Prague, from Prague (whence he fled the Nazi invasion) to Copenhagen and then Oslo (1939), Stockholm and Upsala (1940) (where he was offered academic positions). He finally settled in New York, where he taught at the Ecole Libre des Hautes Etudes created by French and Belgian refugees, before being summoned to Columbia University and then MIT. Always at home in numerous languages, he said of himself: 'I speak Russian in nineteen languages'.

– his enormously varied interests (and skills). Although primarily a specialist in poetics and phonology, his interests throughout a scientific career spanning sixty years led him to general linguistics, translation, literature and poetics, folklore, ethnography, the acquisition and loss of language, glossolalia. . . More than two hundred researchers contributed to the Festschrift devoted to him on his seventieth birthday (*To Honor Roman Jakobson*, 1966).

– his talents as a founder and organizer, which led him to participate in the creation of numerous Circles (Moscow, Prague, inspirer of Copenhagen and New York) and reviews (*Travaux Linguistique de Prague* in 1927, *Acta Linguistica* in 1939, *Word* in 1945), and to stimulate enormous debates wherever he went.

His conception of *langue* was always influenced by literature and art: 'What must have primarily influenced my approach to poetics and linguistics was my proximity to the poets and painters of the avant-garde'.[38] The European phases of his itinerant existence were marked by frequent contact with painters and poets (Malevitch, Mayakovsky, Khlebnikov, Pasternak, Elsa Triolet, the Briks in Russia; Nezval, Seifert, Teige in Czechoslovakia). By contrast, the American phase was characterized by his association with scientists – the physicist Niels Bohr, the biologist François Jacob, the neurologist Luria, the cybernetician Wiener, the analytical philosopher Quine and the semiotican Peirce (of whom Jakobson remarked that he was 'the most powerful source of inspiration' he had found in the United States). His friendship with Trubetzkoy in Prague was the crucible from which phonology emerged, and this linked him to Lévi-Strauss in New York from 1942 onwards, with a decisive impact on the expansion of structuralism outside the domain of linguistics.

Jakobson acknowledged numerous very diverse influences, but throughout his career affirmed the importance of the CGL: 'The five subsequent decades have witnessed an unprecedented, strenuous rise and capital revision of the linguistic science, and the clearest way to point out the essential innovations will be to confront them with the Saussarian doctrine which has been viewed as the start of a new era in the science of language.'[39]

However, it would appear that he was possibly more interested in the reflection it stimulated than the actual doctrinal corpus itself. For there was not a single Saussurian concept that he did not subject to more or less radical criticism – starting with the very notion of the indispensability of the antinomies to the demarcation of the object of linguistics: gradual efforts to bridge and synthesize these "inner dualities" . . . mark the post-Saussurian stage of linguistics'.[40] This challenged Saussure's conception of an object specific to the linguist, and since the dichotomies were not recognized as an exclusionary device criticism of them one by one became possible.

The idea of the arbitrariness of the sign was gradually revised, in favour of a motivation of the bond between signifier and signified. The linearity of the signifier was called into question by the analysis of phonemes into distinctive features. Consequent upon the critique of the arbitrariness of the sign, the non-pertinence of substance to the study of form was rejected. The *langue/parole* dichotomy was abolished ('analysis of the code takes account of messages and vice versa'), as was that of synchrony/diachrony ('linguistic changes partake of a dynamic synchrony'). The two axes were preserved, but so revised that the paradigmatic could accommodate the marked/unmarked opposition; they would later be redefined as metaphor and metonymy. Even the distinction between internal linguistics and external linguistics gave way before Jakobson's interest in external linguistics: 'the determination of the socio-cultural framework of language and historical work that this entails is a necessary complement to the comprehensive analysis of the internal structure of language'.[41] Saussure's architecture in its entirety could scarcely be more contested.

Moreover, throughout his life Jakobson maintained an idea which not only owes nothing to Saussure, but indeed represents a quite different linguistic logic: the notion of 'functions of language'. Jakobson's commitment to it extends from the somewhat simplistic opposition between ordinary language and poetic language introduced by Russian Formalism, through the pragmatic functions inspired by Bühler's three terms (representative, expressive and appelative functions) – to which the Prague linguists added the poetic function – up to the elaboration of the

schema of communication inspired by Shannon and Weaver'
information theory, in which he distinguishes six function
(referential, expressive, conative, phatic, metalinguistic an
poetic) depending on which factor of communication i
predominant.[42]

Apparently so un-Saussurian, why did Jakobson remai
attached to Saussure? There is only one possible answe
Jakobson discovered in the CGL the principle of difference
which provides access to the system, and permanently adopte
it for the study of *langue*.

'The question of invariance in the midst of variation has bee
the dominant topic and methodological device underlying m
diversified yet homogeneous research work'.[43] This was ho
Jakobson encapsulated the key to his work. It could be turne
into a structuralist slogan – 'discovering the invariants amon
all this variety'.[44]

Since his reflections led him to the frontiers of the othe
human sciences, Jakobson required a representation of th
relations between disciplines, which he conceived as a group o
concentric circles:

biological sciences of communication
anthropological sciences of communication
semiotics
linguistics

Jakobson's theoretical profile therefore seems much more likel
to appeal to the human sciences than an exclusionary theor
like Saussure's.

Moreover, it was frequently Jakobson's presentation c
general linguistics, and especially semiotics (he adopted th
American term), that influenced the structuralists. And just a
he continued to salute Saussure as his basic inspiration, so the
declared themselves Saussurians whilst being Jakobsonians.

5.2 Because 'language exists'

Over and above fundamental influences, it is futile attempting t
identify the paths by which the future structuralists discovere
Jakobson and Saussure. It will simply be recalled that from th

eginning of the 1950s reference to them became ever more equent.

Ethnology, psychoanalysis, archaeology of knowledge, philos- ohy, epistemology, literary criticism, Marxism... In the sence of any common objective, what, aside from temporal incidence, united the structuralists in these various fields and hat justification is there for considering them to be part of the me movement? And how to characterize that movement?

'Expanded' or 'generalized' structuralism was essentially rench. This is not the place to ask why, although it is possible identify elements in the philosophical and social-scientific njuncture at the beginning of the 1950s which permit a sponse. Our concern is not with structuralism in general, and e shall restrict ourselves to examining the relation of these orks to linguistics.

Despite profound dissimilarities, they do possess a unifying rinciple: in their various ways, they perceive themselves in a ertain relation to language, discourse, linguistics, structural nguistics, or Saussurian linguistics. 'For all those people, nguage exists', Barthes was to say in a posthumously televized terview in 1988; it exists and constitutes a subject for reflec- on in itself. This was a decisive point of rupture with existen- alism and the immediately preceding period.

The reference to Saussure took various forms: strict appli- ation of the structural method and phonology (Lévi-Strauss); tilization of particular elements without concern for the whole roblematic (Lacan); selection of some concepts in conjunction ith numerous other contributions (Barthes); rejection of the roblematic of the sign as a site of phonocentrism (Derrida); heer absence, as in Foucault and Althusser, for whom the elation to language derived, not from linguistics, but from the xt and especially the letter of the text.

One of several possible axes of differentiation, reference to aussure serves to indicate the extreme heterogeneity of the urrent and obliges us to distinguish various levels among the heories bearing the name of 'structuralism'. Three will be istinguished here, leading to the identification of two different henomena in what has until now been called 'expanded tructuralism':

149

– structural linguistics, generally attributed to Saussure as a partially phantasized founding father figure;

– semiology, or structuralism in the restricted sense. The concepts it advances often have Saussurian names. But there are others too, and the transmission to the human sciences mainly occurred via Jakobson and Hjelmslev's reconstructions. The typical representatives of this current are Lévi-Strauss and Barthes in the period from *Mythologies* (1957) to the beginning of the 1970s (at which point a method applicable to everything loses its attraction for him and he returns to texts).

– structuralism in the broad sense, better understood as philosophical context than as method, and comprising such diverse œuvres as Lacanian psychoanalysis, Foucault's archaeology of knowledge and Derrida's grammatology, which are mainly linked by their common rejection of existentialism, psychology and the reductive use made of phenomenology in France.

Our survey will stop at semiology, for structuralism in the broad sense pertains more to a historical or philosophical study and its connection to our starting-point – Saussure – becomes extremely tenuous.

5.3 The real structuralists: Lévi-Strauss and Barthes

New York, 1942. At the Ecole des Hautes Etudes de New York, Jakobson gives a series of lectures in French on the subject of the phoneme, later published as *Six Lectures on Sound and Meaning* (1976). In the audience is the French anthropologist Claude Lévi-Strauss, a professor at the Ecole. Thirty years later Lévi-Strauss will write the preface to Jakobson's book and reveal how their meeting shattered his previous conception of his discipline.

There is little difference in tone between Lévi-Strauss's first articles on structural anthropology (e.g., 'Structural Analysis in Linguistics and Anthropology' (1945)), shot through with a naive enthusiasm, and his comments thirty years on. In 1945 he wrote: 'A linguistic journal like *Word* . . . must also welcome psychologists, sociologists, and anthropologists eager to learn from modern linguistics the road which leads to the empirical knowledge of social phenomena'.[45] Lévi-Strauss received the 'revelation' of Saussure and Trubetzkoy from Jakobson. His starting-point is Trubetzkoy's programmatic statement of 1933, which singles out four characteristics of phonology:

– it passes from the study of conscious linguistic phenomena to study of their unconscious infrastructure;

– it declines to treat terms as independent entities, concentrating instead on their relations;

– these relations operate within a system;

– it aims at the discovery of general laws.

The analogy is postulated immediately: 'Although they belong to *another order of reality*, kinship phenomena are *of the same type* as linguistic phenomena'. Accordingly, it is possible to apply to them a 'method analogous *in form*'.[46] The *découpage* effected by a system inside a potentially unlimited material (phonic or social) is comparable; the terms which only have value through their relations are comparable.

Lévi-Strauss was later to push the analogy even further: 'Just like the phoneme, which though it has no meaning of its own serves as a means by which meanings can be formed, the incest prohibition seemed to me to be the link connecting two domains hitherto held to be divorced from each other.'[47] Just as phonemes only possess value through their oppositional relations, so any kinship system is characterized by two fundamental terms (man/woman) entering into relations of alliance, filiation and consanguinity. The aspect of the linguistic system highlighted here is the primacy of the system over the terms. The comparison is extended to myths, which are likewise 'composed of elements which are combined together to form meanings without in themselves, considered in isolation, signifying anything'.[48] Lévi-Strauss goes so far as to coin the curious neologism 'mytheme', constituent unit of the myth.

Presented thus, the analogy appears something of a caricature. More interesting is the fact that Lévi-Strauss showed himself capable of producing results with it. Taking up Radcliffe-Brown's analysis of the avuncular relationship, for example, he demonstrated that Radcliffe-Brown was unable to account for it because of his failure to relate it to the whole of the familial system, because he failed to conceive it as a structure.

If there is a connection between Roland Barthes and Lévi-Strauss, it is in so far as Barthes too takes the propositions of structural linguistics sufficiently seriously to derive an immediately utilizable methodology from them.

As he recalled in the preface to a new edition of *Mythologies* in 1970, Barthes only began to read Saussure in 1957: 'I had just read Saussure and as a result acquired the conviction that by treating "collective representations" as sign-systems, one might hope to go further than the pious show of unmasking them'.[49] Three phases in Barthe's use of semiology should be distinguished:

– the first is exemplified by *Mythologies* and the theoretical text which follows, 'Myth Today'. Here Barthes only appeals to a few elements of the linguistic conceptual apparatus: sign, signifier and signified (adopted from Saussure) and the Hjelmslevian distinctions between denotation and connotation and between language-object and metalanguage. This period is very productive, and speaking of the seventy or so articles he wrote between 1957 and 1963 Barthes was subsequently to remember a veritable 'methodological enchantment' faced with the enormous work programme that presented itself.

– *The Fashion System* (1967), conceived as concomitant with the theoretical text *Elements of Semiology* (1964), represents an authentic utilization of the notion of system, of the primacy of the system over the elements, and of difference. Barthes had discovered Lévi-Strauss, Trubetzkoy (whose comparison betwen phonology and the study of dress delighted him), and Jakobson (from whom he made only a few terminological borrowings – e.g., 'shifter' – in the first instance). Characterizing these two phases, Barthes referred to an initial semiological period – a taxonomic phase – which he was later to view as a static, 'naive project'.

– To these two phases Barthes counterposed a third, in which he resumed thinking about dynamic and historical phenomena. For him this was the period of semiology's maturity, involving a broader epistemological reflection. By returning to literature above all, he progressively added new concepts to those hitherto at work – extending connotation, for example, to plural readings, thus facilitating study of the pole of reception. Parallel to

Barthes' work, in the course of the 1960s Julia Kristeva, Gérard Genette, Jacques Derrida, Tzvetan Todorov (French translator and introducer of the Russian Formalists), and the Italian Umberto Eco demonstrated the productive capacity of structuralism with respect even to so subtle an object as literature, in analyses that avoided any mere application of linguistics.

The 1950s saw a generalization of the reference to Saussure, including among people who did not attempt a structuralist application of his work. The philosopher Maurice Merleau-Ponty was the first to evoke the sign and Saussure in 1953, in his inaugural lecture at the Collège de France: 'The theory of the sign, as elaborated by linguistics, may imply a theory of historical meaning which can cut across the alternative of *things* or *consciousness*... Saussure may well have sketched a new philosophy of history.'[50] Merleau-Ponty was to play a major role in the diffusion of the reference to Saussure in the 1950s; the subsequent philosophical generalization is partly due to him.

.4 From language to the subject

By adopting progressive distance from Saussure as a classificatory principle, we can assign the other 'structuralists' to two groups: on the one hand, Lacan and Derrida, who genuinely use aspects of Saussure's text; on the other hand, Foucault and Althusser, who are structuralists in a sense which no longer has anything to do with structural linguistics.

In Lacan and Derrida it is possible briefly to locate traces of a relation to Saussure.

Two periods can be distinguished in Lacan's reading of Saussure. The first, up to the 'Rome Discourse' of 1953, remains a passive reading, influenced by Lévi-Strauss. Then, between 1953 and 1963, Lacan conducts a new reading in the light of Jakobson, whom he cites almost as often as Saussure. This enables him to accomplish a veritable reconstruction of the Freudian conceptual system. The fecundity of this period is evident in 'The Agency of the Letter' (1957), where his reflection on the sign and the signifier lead him, by his utilization of the notion of value, to highlight the fact that any signification always refers to another. Contemporaneously with Jakobson's 'Two Aspects of Language and Two Types of

Aphasic Disturbances', he employs the relationship between the two axes of metaphor and metonymy to conceptualize the language-like [*langagier*] functioning of the unconscious (which allows him to advance the thesis that 'the unconscious is structured like a language'). Thus Lacan's approach involves a few elements from the Saussurian system reworked in accordance with his own perspective; moreover, the reference to Saussure will become more and more remote in the seminars, from the 1960s onwards.

As to Derrida, he explicitly criticizes Saussure's theory of the sign, seeking to reveal its links with a certain metaphysics (phonocentrism as logocentrism). In order to liberate the semiological project from a linguistics founded upon phonologism, he proposes to recast 'semiology' as 'grammatology'. Here Saussure is nothing more than a rejected reference point.[51]

Notwithstanding the importance they accord to the CGL, then, both authors can only be designated 'structuralists' by a very liberal use of the term.

In the case of Foucault and Althusser the metaphor is even stronger: there is no question of searching for references to Saussure in their work. One might simply say that the structuralist climate had an impact upon it at a certain point (the middle of the 1960s), as Althusser's foreword to a new edition of *Reading Capital* in 1968 testifies: 'Despite the precautions we took to distinguish ourselves from the "structuralist" ideology ... despite the decisive intervention of categories foreign to "structuralism" ... the terminology we employed was too close in many respects to the "structuralist" terminology not to give rise to an ambiguity.'[52]

Recognition of the heterogeneity of the structuralists brings us back to what has been regarded as their common ground: the reference to language. Another point in common would be the effect of language on their conception of the subject. For all of them the subject is dissolved in language since, however far back one goes, language is always anterior.

But the point at which they definitively part company into two groups, leading anglophone commentators to contrast 'structuralism' and 'post-structuralism', is the use made of this language always-already there. In Barthes or Lévi-Strauss the transfer of essentially unreconstructed concepts from linguistics results in the preservation of the idea of a human nature as a specific object and an explanatory principle. By contrast, Lacan, Derrida, Foucault and Althusser reject such a conception of the subject, and their so-called 'anti-humanism' amounts to the abandonment of transcendental subjectification: the fact that language is always-already there defines the subject as position, but never as substance.

Is it necessary to conclude with a balance-sheet?
We have seen that if one takes Saussure's theory term by term, little passes into linguistic posterity as such. If it is asked what remains of Saussure in expanded structuralism, the answer is – scarcely more than an attention to language shared by all linguists. So was the influence he exerted no more than an imaginary heritage? No: he made a fair proportion of the twentieth century think.

3. Bibliography to Part Two

The fate of Saussurian texts and concepts
De Mauro, Tullio *Introduzione e annotazione all'edizione italiana del Cours de linguistique générale* di Ferdinand de Saussure, Editori Laterza, Bari 1967.
Engler, Rudolf, 'Théorie et critique d'un principe saussurien: l'arbitraire du signe', *Cahiers Ferdinand de Saussure* 19, 1962.
——, 'Le Destin des Antinomies', *Cahiers Ferdinand de Saussure* 22, 1966.
——, 'Biliographie saussurienne', *Cahiers Ferdinand de Saussure* 30, 31, 34 and 40, 1976–.
Godel, Robert, 'Problèmes de linguistique saussurienne', *Cahiers Ferdinand de Saussure* 29, 1974.
Hjelmslev, Louis, 'Essai d'une théorie des morphèmes' (1936), *Actes du 4ème Congrès International des Linguistes*, Copenhagen, 1938, Kraus Reprint.
Koerner, Ernst F. K., *Bibliographia Saussureana (1870–1970). An Annotated, Classified Bibliography on the Background, Development and Actual Relevance of Ferdinand de Saussure's General Theory of Language*, Scarecrow Press, Metuchen (N.J.) 1972.
——, *Ferdinand de Saussure, Origin and Development of his Linguistic Thought in Western Studies of Language: A Contribution to the History and Theory of Linguistics*, Vieweg, Braunschweig 1973.

Meillet, Antoine, 'Compte-rendu du Cours de Linguistique Générale', *Bulletin de la Société Linguistique de Paris* 64, 1916.

Séchehaye, Albert, 'Les Problèmes de la langue à la lumière d'une théorie nouvelle', *Revue Philosophique*, Volume 84, 1917.

Linguistic structuralism (general)

Actes du Premier Congrès International des Linguistes (1928), A. W. Sijthoff, Leiden 1930.

Benveniste, Emile, *Problèmes de linguistique générale I*, Gallimard, Paris 1966.

——, *Problèmes de linguistique générale II*, Gallimard, Paris 1974.

Bronckart, Jean-Pierre, *Théories du langage, une introduction critique*, Mardaga, Brussels 1977.

Ducrot, Oswald, 'Le Structuralisme en linguistique', *Qu'est-ce que le structuralisme?* Seuil, Paris 1966.

—— and Todorov, Tzvetan, *Encyclopedic Dictionary of the Sciences of Language* (1972), Basil Blackwell, Oxford 1979 (especially the articles on Saussurianism, Glossematics, Functionalism, Distributionalism, Generative Linguistics, Sign, Syntagma and Paradigm, Language and Speech, Arbitrariness, Synchrony and Diachrony).

Gadet, Françoise and Pêcheux, Michel, *La Langue introuvable*, Maspero, Paris 1981.

Jakobson, Roman, *Selected Writings, Volume One – Phonological Studies*, Mouton, The Hague 1971.

——, 'An Example of Migratory Terms and Institutional Modes (on the Fiftieth Anniversary of the Moscow Linguistic Circle)', *Selected Writings, Volume Two – Word and Language*, Mouton, The Hague 1971.

Lepschy, Giulio, *A Survey of Structural Linguistics* (1962), Deutsch, London 1982.

Ricoeur, Paul, 'La Structure, le mot, l'événement', *Esprit*, May 1967.

Ruwet, Nicolas, 'La Linguistique générale aujourd'hui', *Archives européennes de sociologie* V, 1964.

The structuralist schools (particular)

Prague

Abaiev, V. I., 'Modernisme et déshumanisation de la linguistique' (1965), *Langages* 15, 1969.

Change, 3, special issue on the Prague Circle.

Jakobson, Roman and Pomorska, Krystyna, *Dialogues* (1980), Cambridge University Press, Cambridge 1983.

——, *Une vie dans le langage*, Minuit, Paris 1985.

Martinet, André, *Economie des changements phonétiques*, Francke, Berne 1955.

Milner, Jean-Claude, 'L'Amour de la langue, entretien', *Action poétique* 72, 1977.

Prieto, Luis J., *Messages et signaux*, Presses Universitaires de France, Paris 1966.

Trubetzkoy, Nicolas, *Principles of Phonology* (1939), University of California Press, Los Angeles and Berkeley 1969.

AN IMAGINARY HERITAGE

Copenhagen

Arrivé, Michel, 'L'Épouvantail du structuralisme', *Dialectiques* 26, 1979.

Greimas, Algirdas J., Préface to Louis Hjelmslev, *Langage*, Minuit, Paris 1966.

Hjelmslev, Louis, *Prolegomena to a Theory of Language* (1943), University of Wisconsin Press, Madison 1961.

——, *Language: An Introduction* (1963), University of Wisconsin Press, Madison 1970.

Meschonnic, Henri, *Le Signe et le poème*, Gallimard, Paris 1975.

Rastier, François, Préface to Louis Hjelmslev, *Nouveaux essais*, Presses Universitaires de France, Paris 1985.

Geneva

Amacker, René, 'L'Influence de Ferdinand de Saussure et la linguistique générale d'inspiration saussurienne en Suisse (1940–1970)', *Cahiers Ferdinand de Saussure* 30, 1976.

Frei, Henri, *La Grammaire des fautes* (1929), Slatkine Republications, Geneva.

Yale

Bloomfield, Leonard, 'Review of the Cours de Linguistique Générale', *Modern Language Journal* 8, 1924.

——, *Language*, Holt, New York 1933.

Harris, Zellig, *Structural Linguistics*, University of Chicago Press, Chicago 1951.

Pike, Kenneth L., *Selected Writings*, Mouton, The Hague 1972.

Wells, R. S., 'De Saussure's System of Linguistics', Word, Vol. 3, Nos. 1–2, 1947.

MIT

Change, 'Hypotheses', Paris 19 .

Chomsky, Noam, *Aspects of the Theory of Syntax*, MIT Press, Cambridge (Mass.) 1965.

——, *Language and Mind*, Harcourt and Brace, New York 1968.

Benveniste

Benveniste, Emile, *Problèmes de linguistique générale*, two volumes, Gallimard, Paris 1966 and 1974.

Maldidier, Denise, 'Quelle sorte d'objet est le sujet de la langue?' *LINX* 13, Paris-X Nanterre 1985.

Normand, Claudine, 'Le Sujet dans la langue', *Langages* 77, 1985.

Jakobson

Holenstein, Elmar, *Roman Jakobson's Approach to Language: Phenomenological Structuralism*, Indiana University Press, Bloomington 1976.

Jakobson, Roman, 'Linguistics and Poetics', in T. A. Sebeok (ed.), *Style in Language*, MIT Press, Cambridge (Mass.) 1960.

——, 'Two Aspects of Language and Two Types of Aphasic Disturbances', in idem and Halle, Morris, *Fundamentals of Language*, Mouton, The Hague 1956.

——, *Six Lectures on Sound and Meaning* (1976), Harvester, Hassocks 1978.

——, *Verbal Art, Verbal Sign, Verbal Time*, Basil Blackwell, Oxford 1985.

Milner, Jean-Claude, 'Jakobson ou le bonheur par la symétrie', in *Ordres et raisons de langue*, Seuil, Paris 1982.

Structuralism outside linguistics

Althusser, Louis and Balibar, Etienne, *Reading Capital* (1968), New Left Books, London 1970.

Arrivé, Michel, 'Signifiant saussurien et signifiant lacanien', *Langages* 77, 1985.

Barthes, Roland, *Mythologies* (1957), Paladin, London 1982.

——, *Elements of Semiology* (1964), Hill and Wang, New York 1968.

——, 'Linguistique et littérature', *Langages* 12, 1968.

——, Interview (1970) by Jean-José Marchand, Emission Océaniques, broadcast February 1988.

Boudon, Raymond, *The Uses of Structuralism* (1968), Heinemann, London 1971.

Broekman, Jan, *Structuralism – Moscow, Prague, Paris*, Reidel, Dordrecht/ Boston 1974.

Calvet, Louis-Jean, *Roland Barthes*, Payot, Paris 1973.

Chiss, Jean-Louis and Puech, Christian, *Les Fondements de la linguistique, études d'histoire et d'épistémologie*, de Boeck-Université, Brussels 1988.

Derrida, Jacques, *Of Grammatology* (1967), The Johns Hopkins University Press, Baltimore 1976.

Descombes, Vincent, *Modern French Philosophy*, Cambridge University Press, Cambridge 1981.

Eco, Umberto, *La struttura assente*, Bompiani, Milan 1968.

Foucault, Michel, *The Archaeology of Knowledge* (1969), Tavistock, London 1974.

Hawkes, Terence, *Structuralism and Semiotics*, Methuen, London 1977.

Henry, Paul, 'Theoretical Issues behind Michel Pêcheux's Analyse automatique du discours', *Konteksten*, Amsterdam 1988.

Lacan, Jacques, 'The Function and Field of Speech and Language in Psychoanalysis' (1956), in *Ecrits: A Selection*, Tavistock, London 1977.

——, 'The Agency of the Letter in the Unconscious or Reason since Freud' (1957), in *Ecrits: A Selection*.

——, 'Radiophonie', *Scilicet* 2/3, Paris 1970.

Lecercle, Jean-Jacques, *Philosophy through the Looking-Glass*, Hutchinson, London 1985.

Lévi-Strauss, Claude, 'Structural Analysis in Linguistics and in Anthropology' (1945), in *Structural Anthropology* (1958), Allen Lane, London 1968.

——, *The Savage Mind* (1962), Weidenfeld and Nicolson, London 1966.

——, Preface to Roman Jakobson, *Six Lectures on Sound and Meaning*, Harvester, Hassocks 1978.

Milner, Jean-Claude, *L'Amour de la langue*, Seuil, Paris 1978.

Piaget, Jean, *Structuralism* (1968), Routledge and Kegan Paul, London 1971.

Pavel, Thomas, *Le Mirage linguistique*, Minuit, Paris 1988.

Propp, Vladimir, *Morphology of the Folktale* (1928), University of Texas Press, Austin 1968.

Robey, David (ed.), *Structuralism: An Introduction*, Oxford University Press, Oxford 1973.

Roudinesco, Elisabeth, *La Bataille de cent ans*, Volume 2, Seuil, Paris 1986.

Safouan, Moustafa, 'De la structure en psychanalyse', *Qu'est-ce que le structuralisme?*, Seuil, Paris 1968.

Sperber, Dan, 'Le Structuralisme en anthropologie', *Qu'est-ce que le structuralisme?*.

Wahl, François, 'Le Structuralisme philosophique', *Qu'est-ce que le structuralisme?*.

Young, Robert (ed.), *Untying the Text: A Poststructuralist Reader*, Routledge and Kegan Paul 1981.

Notes to Part One

1. A Strange Master

1. This is true, at any rate, of Benveniste, Martinet, Hjelmslev, Jespersen, Jakobson, Bloomfield, Chomsky and Labov.
2. For example, those by Lacan, Lévi-Strauss, Barthes, Safouan, Mannoni, Bourdieu, Derrida and Ricoeur (to speak only of France).
3. Chomsky is the founder of generative grammar. In the course of elaborating it, he both acknowledged the significance of structuralism and argued the possibility of superseding it. His first texts often discuss Saussure. *Current Issues in Linguistic Theory* (1964) reveals that Chomsky also took an interest in the sources (v. the references to Godel). This does not prevent his reading from being prejudiced.
4. In other words, the Saussure of the anagrams. This idea of Saussurian duality can be found, *inter alia*, in Louis-Jean Calvet, *Pour et contre Saussure* (Paris 1975) (for the Saussure of the anagrams, against the Saussure of the CGL).
5. In order to explain an otherwise incomprehensible phenomenon, in the *Mémoire* Saussure assumed the existence in Indo-European of a sound of which no known language contained a trace. After his death the decipherment of Hittite revealed the existence of the phoneme, whose exact nature and role Saussure had deduced. Hence he belongs to the company of scientists who, rather than confining themselves to the empirical, have employed a hypothetico-deductive method. The *Mémoire* rapidly made Saussure famous in the comparatist world, and for many linguists in the first half of the twentieth century (e.g., Meillet or Benveniste in the 1950s) was the work that qualified him as a major linguist.
6. Among the principal comparatist theoreticians in Leipzig were Brugmann and Osthoff, who displayed a certain malevolence in their reception of the *Mémoire*.
7. The precise reasons for Saussure's departure remain an obscure point of his biography – as does the progressive silence which followed his

160

return to Geneva. On the fiftieth anniversary of his death, Benveniste was to write: 'What a mystery surrounds his life, which soon receded into silence' (*Problèmes de linguistique générale*, Gallimard, Paris 1966, p. 32).

8. The French editions published since 1970 include a translation of these notes.

9. The expression is Jakobson's. In Calvet, op. cit., p. 107, one finds 'genuine Saussurian revolution' ('genuine', because he denies the CGL revolutionary status). This 'second Saussure' was developed in several works – e.g., 'The Two Saussures', *Semiotexte* I, 2, 1974 and II, 1, 1975.

10. The term appears to occur for the first time in Giulio C. Lepschy's *A Survey of Structural Linguistics* (published in 1962). Thereafter it has been unanimously accepted by commentators who oppose the vulgate in the name of the sources. It is worth noting that the vulgate is always attributed to other people; no-one ever admits to being a supporter of it.

2. How the *Course in General Linguistics* was Constructed

1. These notes, described in the *Sources manuscrites*, were published by Godel in *Cahiers Ferdinand de Saussure* 12.

2. When reference is made to Engler, it will be in the form 2115 E (extract 2115, column E).

   Where possible, extracts will always be cited from the CGL. Where a source is concerned, it will be cited either from Engler or Godel, or, if it does not feature in either, from another edition.

3. One cannot resist the comparison with another body of thought whose transmission was not ensured by writing: Lacan's Seminars. However, a big difference is that the tape recorder had not been invented in 1910.

4. Cf. the same image in the interview with Gautier (quoted on p. 20). For the meaning of the terms used by Saussure, see Chapter 4.

5. 'This volume' refers to a book planned in 1894, but never written.

6. De Mauro provides the elements for such a reconstruction; see note 65 of his commentary on the CGL.

7. De Mauro (p. 409) suggests an interesting parallel with the difficulties encountered by another philosopher of language, Wittgenstein, with this same problem of presentation (e.g., in the Introduction to the *Philosophical Investigations*). Wittgenstein adopted the form of 'philosophical remarks', whereas Saussure renounced the idea of writing altogether.

3. The Sign

1. The editors only succeed in exacerbating the contradiction in the formulation with their addition of the arrows and such comments as 'each [element] recalls the others', which suggests that the elements pre-exist each other and await their counterpart. But the responsibility for the contradiction cannot be attributed exclusively to them; it derives from Saussure's own equivocations.

4. The System

1. The question of identity was a major preoccupation of Saussure's, and also features in his discussion of the legends of the *Nibelungen*: 'All the incongruities of thought derive from insufficient reflection on the nature of *identity* or the characteristics of identity when non-living beings are involved, like *words, mythical figures*, or a *letter of the alphabet* – all of which are simply different forms of the SIGN, in the philosophical sense' (SM, p. 136).

5. The Object

1. Note that the adjective *linguistic* corresponds to the three nouns *langage*, *langue* and *linguistics* – whence numerous ambiguities.
2. Noam Chomsky, *Aspects of the Theory of Syntax*, Cambridge (Mass.) 1965, p. 4.

7. The Play of the Signifier

1. Anagram, hypogram, paragram. . . Saussure hesitated a long time over what to call the phenomenon.
2. This was the name adopted by Mlle Smith in her Hindu 'novel'.
3. French linguist of the late nineteenth and early twentieth century, author in particular of *Le Langage martien* (1901).
4. In *Theories of the Symbol* (Oxford 1982) p. 260, Todorov notes a highly significant *lapsus*, which reveals that Saussure in fact came very close to understanding the problem of the relation to the mother tongue. Commenting upon his specimen of 'Latinoid', he writes: 'the text does not confuse *two* languages. Although the words are scarcely Latin, at least we see no *third* language . . . intervene'. *Two* languages, then *three*? What could the third be – if not the excluded mother tongue?

5. An added reason for saluting their theoretical honesty.
6. The proximity of the two phenomena is further underscored by the fact that *durchbläuen*, which illustrates association by the signifier in Course III, illustrates folk etymology in Course I.

Notes to Part Two

1. Robert Young, Introduction to idem (ed.), *Untying the Text: A Post-Structuralist Reader*, London 1981, p. 1.
2. Emile Benveniste, *Problèmes de linguistique générale II*, Paris 1974, p. 16.
3. Antoine Meillet, 'Compte-rendu du Cours de Linguistique Générale', *Bulletin de la Société Linguistique de Paris* 64, 1916, pp. 49–51.
4. Albert Séchehaye, 'Les Problèmes de la langue á la lumière d'une théorie nouvelle', *Revue Philosophique*, volume 84, 1917.
5. V. I. Abaiev, 'Modernisme et déshumanisation de la linguistique', *Langages* 15, 1969.
6. Jacques Lacan, *Ecrits: A Selection*, London 1977, p. 298.
7. Roman Jakobson, *Selected Writings*, Volume II, The Hague 1971, p. 534.
8. Henri F. Muller, 'Word', *Word*, Vol. 1, no. 1, 1945, pp. 3–4.
9. Jakobson, op. cit., p. 538.
10. *Change* 3,
11. 'Thèses présentées au Premier Congrès des philologues slaves', reprinted in Josef Vachek, *A Prague School Reader in Linguistics*, Bloomington 1964, pp. 33–4.
12. Jean-Claude Milner, 'L'Amour de la langue, entretien', *Action poétique* 72, 1977, p. 91.
13. See Jakobson, op. cit., pp. 3–15.
14. A. -J. Greimas, Préface to Louis Hjelmslev, *Le Langage, une introduction*, Paris 1966, p. 12.
15. Michel Arrivé, 'L'Épouvantail du structuralisme', *Dialectiques* 26, 1979.
16. Nicolas Ruwet, 'La Linguistique générale aujourd'hui', *Archives européennes de sociologie* V, 1964.
17. Louis Hjelmslev, *Prolegomena to a Theory of Language*, Madison 1961, p. 58.
18. François Rastier, Préface to Louis Hjelmslev, *Nouveaux essais*, Paris 1985, p. 8.
19. Michel Arrivé, art. cit., p. 38.

20. Henri Meschonnic, *Le Signe et le poème*, Paris 1975, p. 231.

21. R. S. Wells, 'De Saussure's System of Linguistics', *Word*, Vol. 3, nos. 1–2, 1947, p. 14.

22. See R. M. Brend (ed.), *Kenneth L. Pike: Selected Writings*, The Hague 1972.

23. See *Change*, pp. 63–71.

24. See Ruwet, art. cit.

25. See 'Les Niveaux de l'analyse linguistique' (1964), in Emile Benveniste, *Problèmes de linguistique générale I*, Paris 1966.

26. Denise Maldidier, 'Quelle sorte d'objet est le sujet de la langue?', *LINX* 13, Paris-X Nanterre 1985, p. 26.

27. See Jean-Claude Milner, 'Jakobson ou le bonheur par la symétrie', in *Ordre et raisons de langue*, Paris 1982, p. 336.

28. Rudolf Engler, 'Le Destin des antinomies', *Cahiers Ferdinand de Saussure* 22, 1966, p. 35.

29. See Rudolf Engler, 'Théorie et critique d'un principe Saussurien: l'arbitraire du signe', *Cahiers Ferdinand de Saussure* 19, 1962, pp. 12ff.

30. Roland Barthes, *Elements of Semiology*, New York 1968, p. 11.

31. Jacques Lacan, 'The Agency of the Letter in the Unconscious or Reason since Freud' (1957), in *Ecrits: A Selection*, London 1977, p. 149.

32. Roman Jakobson, *Selected Writings*, Volume II, p. 717.

33. Roman Jakobson, *Selected Writings*, Volume I, The Hague 1971, p. 420.

34. Louis Hjelmslev, 'Essai d'une théorie des morphèmes', *Actes du 4ème Congrès International des Linguistes*, Copenhagen 1938.

35. In Roman Jakobson and Morris Halle, *Fundamentals of Language*, The Hague 1956.

36. Jacques Lacan, 'Radiophonie', *Scilicet* 2/3, Paris 1970, p. 62.

37. Roland Barthes, 'Linguistique et littérature', *Langages* 12, 1968, p. 4.

38. Roman Jakobson, 'My Favorite Topics', in idem, *Verbal Art, Verbal Sign, Verbal Time*, Oxford 1985, p. 7.

39. Roman Jakobson, *Selected Writings*, Volume II, pp. 716–17.

40. Ibid, p. 717.

41. Roman Jakobson and Krystyna Pomorska, *Dialogues*, Cambridge 1983, pp. 156–57.

42. See Roman Jakobson, 'Linguistics and Poetics', in T. A. Sebeok (ed.), *Style in Language*, Cambridge (Mass.) 1960.

43. Roman Jakobson, 'My Favorite Topics', p. 3.

44. Roman Jakobson, *Six Lectures on Sound and Meaning*, Hassocks 1978, p. 10.

45. Claude Lévi-Strauss, *Structural Anthropology*, Harmondsworth 1977, p. 31.

46. Ibid., p. 34.

47. Claude Lévi-Strauss, Preface to Roman Jakobson, *Six Lectures on Sound and Meaning*, Hassocks 1978, p. xviii.

48. Ibid., p. xxi.
49. Roland Barthes, *Mythologies*, London 1982, p. 9.
50. Quoted in Vincent Descombes, *Modern French Philosophy*, Cambridge 1981, p. 71.
51. See especially Jacques Derrida, *Of Grammatology*, Baltimore 1976.
52. Louis Althusser and Etienne Balibar, *Reading Capital*, London 1970, p. 7.

Index

INDEX

INDEX